Air War Over America

Sept. 11 alters face
of air defense mission

Leslie Filson

HEADQUARTERS 1ST AIR FORCE
PUBLIC AFFAIRS OFFICE
TYNDALL AIR FORCE BASE, FL
2003

Library of Congress Control Number 2003092920
ISBN 0-615-12416-X

Acknowledgments

When 1st Air Force public affairs officer Maj. Don Arias approached me about writing a book on America's air sovereignty mission and how Sept. 11, 2001, changed everything, I was a little nervous.

How do you tell such a huge, multifaceted story in only a few short chapters? Can you ever give a story of this magnitude justice? I really don't know if you can. All you can do is write the stories you think the reader absolutely must know to get a clear picture of all the changes affecting the mission. Speaking of pictures, how do you gather those essential shots that tell a story all by themselves? Thankfully, Maj. Arias enlisted the help of New Mexico Air National Guardsman and historian Master Sgt. Rod Grunwald, a great photo editor, sounding board, copy editor, grammarian, and wordsmith who gathered countless photos for this project. Thank you for all your help, Rod.

Before I go down the professional list, there's many people I want to thank on a personal level. My biggest thank-you of all goes to my husband and on-site aviation consultant, Mike, who spent endless hours at the park with our daughter, Isabel, while I was sequestered in the office writing a book. There's no way I could have done it without Mike, who had to listen to every single detail about this book every single day for more than a year. Thanks for enduring it all, Mike. I also thank my mom, Paula; sisters Alyson and Betsy; and the rest of my family for helping me get through this as we were all trying to get through losing our dad and hero, John. A firefighter and U.S. Marine Corps Vietnam veteran, he would have loved this story of America's military protecting our homeland.

There are many others to thank for supporting this project. First, I thank retired Col. William A. Scott — an outstanding editor — for his sound opinion, advice and valuable input. Col. Scott had the answers to any and all questions from, *"What's a 'conehead'?"* to *"What's Posse Comitatus?"* I truly appreciate all the time you gave, Col. Scott. I am also indebted to retired Maj. Gen. Larry K. Arnold, who wanted this story forever preserved in print. Thank you for your valuable time and many interviews. Special recognition also goes to Col. Bob Marr, commander of the Northeast Air Defense Sector, who gave freely of his time to help with the smallest of details about the air battle on Sept. 11, 2001. Thank you, Col. Marr.

I owe many thanks to the 1st Air Force and Continental United States North American Aerospace Defense Command Region public affairs staff: Maj. Brenda Barker; Staff Sgt. Scott Farley; Master Sgt. Roger Tibbetts; and most of all, Maj. Arias. You were all nothing but supportive through this entire endeavor and Staff Sgt. Farley's editing skills and technical expertise were invaluable!

Several others wholeheartedly supported this project: Lt. Col. Kacey Blaney; retired Brig. Gen. John Broman; Col. John Cromwell; Dr. Charles Gross; Master Sgt. Dale Hanson; Eric Hehs; retired Col. Connie Mac Hostetler; Marty Isham; retired Chief Master Sgt. Bill Johnson; Col. Larry Kemp; Bard Manthey; Dr. Paul McAllister; Maj. Gen. Craig R. McKinley; Gene McManus; Staff Sgt. Mark Morgan; retired Col. Dan Navin; Jerry Schroeder; Master Sgt. Dave Somdahl; Karen Steele; Dr. Rick Sturdevant; Master Sgt. Don Taggart; Brig. Gen. Dave Wherley Jr.; Col. Don Whitehead; Vivian Wilson; and Bob Wright. My sincerest gratitude.

Finally, thank you to the men and women of 1st Air Force and CONR. We can all sleep better knowing you are guarding America's skies.

— Leslie Filson

Foreword

Most Americans remember where they were the morning of Sept. 11, 2001, and will probably never forget. I was in my command center watching live CNN coverage of smoke billowing from the north tower of the World Trade Center, having just scrambled F-15s out of Cape Cod, Mass., toward the possibly hijacked American Airlines Flight 11. When I saw United Airlines Flight 175 hit the south tower, I quickly began to realize this was not a coincidence, that our country was under attack and it was my job to defend against further attacks. Over the next several hours, the men and women of CONR — the Continental United States North American Aerospace Defense Command Region — quickly went about the business of securing America's skies. I am grateful for what they did that day.

We were able to respond quickly Sept. 11 because we had a robust command and control structure in place and some fighter aircraft on rapid reaction alert. The air defense mission, as reflected in the number of fighter aircraft and alert locations, had shrunk over the decades even in the face of the Cold War. To a point, this reduction was justified as the Soviet threat changed from bombers in the 1950s to primarily an Intercontinental Ballistic Missile and submarine ballistic missile threat in the years to follow. Throughout the 1970s and 1980s, the Soviets flew repeated reconnaissance missions off the East Coast of the United States and also developed cruise missile capabilities that posed a threat to the United States. These two facts alone may have kept the air defense and air sovereignty missions alive against air-breathing targets.

With the collapse of the Berlin Wall in 1989 and subsequent dissolution of the Warsaw Pact and the Soviet Union, there was additional pressure to take down our alert aircraft and use that money for other

Photo by Eric Hehs, Code One magazine

Retired Maj. Gen. Larry K. Arnold was commander of 1st Air Force and the Continental United States NORAD Region on Sept. 11, 2001.

Air Force priorities. Only through strong leadership and determination by Gen. Howell M. Estes III, then commander in chief of NORAD, was this country able to sustain any modicum of air sovereignty and air defense. It is important to note that Maj. Gen. Philip G. Killey, the Air National Guard general officer in command of 1st Air Force and CONR during those years, fueled the flame that helped focus Gen. Estes' determination.

When I became the 1st Air Force vice commander in January 1997, the Department of Defense had just released its Quadrennial Defense Review. This document indicated that the Air Force would provide only four fighter alert sites for a "four-corners defense." It was a familiar basketball strategy that had no place in the air sovereignty

U.S. Air Force photo by Staff Sgt. Greg L. Davis

Aircraft maintenance personnel from Shaw Air Force Base, S.C., work on an F-16 late into the night of Sept. 11, 2001. Military personnel from throughout the country were called into action that day as the 14 fighter aircraft on alert exceeded 400 fighter, tanker and Airborne Warning and Control System aircraft just hours after the attacks.

mission. The QDR also called for the reduction of several intermediate Air Force headquarters. Though none of the intermediate headquarters was specifically mentioned in the QDR, 1st Air Force was one of the headquarters on the chopping block. It was only through the actions of Gen. Estes and Maj. Gen. Killey that 1st Air Force continued to exist. Seven fighter alert sites were salvaged — down from 12 in 1993 and 19 in 1991. When Gen. Richard B. Myers became commander of NORAD in 1998, he told the chairman of the Joint Chiefs of Staff that he could provide air sovereignty in name only. He didn't get any more forces.

This was the situation in which we found ourselves on Sept. 11: We had a minimum number of fighters on alert scattered about the country but a well-trained and dedicated command and control system. We took our job seriously, and in briefing after briefing, reiterated that we believed the greatest threat to the United States was an attack by terrorists, rogues or rogue nations.

In the immediate aftermath of the Sept. 11 attack, we were able to provide command and control of air power over the entire continental United States because the mission had been spared. In 18 hours, we surged from 14 aircraft on alert at seven locations to more than 400 fighter, tanker and Airborne Warning and Control System aircraft on orbit and on alert at more than 60 locations. This was a remarkable job, performed by remarkable people at a remarkable time in our nation's history.

— **Retired Maj. Gen. Larry K. Arnold,**
1st Air Force commander,
December 1997 - July 2002

Introduction

On the morning of Sept. 11, 2001, 14 U.S. Air Force fighters stood alert at seven locations in the Continental United States North American Aerospace Defense Command Region. Aircrews surveyed the glorious fall weather from their alert facilities, updated local airfield conditions, reviewed their Air Tasking Orders, preflighted their aircraft missiles, and maybe enjoyed their first cup of coffee.

In the region's three air defense sectors, air battle managers and technicians sat in darkened rooms, peering into radar scopes aglow with the pulsing green dots of radar returns from aircraft entering the continental United States Air Defense Identification Zone. Region Air Operations Center personnel surveyed sector and NORAD activities and monitored the status of regional radars and communications.

It was a typical morning all-around for a small, tight-knit group of people in a largely unknown and little-acknowledged air sovereignty community.

As this team quietly labored to protect the country from external airborne threats, many Americans cast a concerned but mostly disengaged eye on the Middle East and its spiraling cycle of *Intifada* violence. More laid an interested gaze on the sports page and the upcoming college football season. The country was at peace.

At 8:46 a.m. Eastern Standard Time, American Airlines Flight 11 was deliberately flown into the north tower of New York's famous World Trade Center, transforming it into a smoking black pyre. The gruesome scene was transmitted live by CNN reporting to a shocked America that "a light aircraft has hit the World Trade Center!" Americans gathered somberly in front of their televisions, watching in morbid curiosity as the tower burned in yet another version of "reality TV." At 9:03 a.m., United Airlines Flight 175 speared through the

Two F-16A air defense fighters of the 178th Fighter Squadron, North Dakota Air National Guard, lead an F-15C assigned to the 27th Fighter Squadron, Langley Air Force Base, Va., in formation during a Combat Air Patrol mission on Nov. 17, 2001.

U.S. Air Force photo by Staff Sgt. Greg L. Davis

south tower, bursting into an incandescent ball of burning jet fuel. Curiosity turned to horror, fascination to fear. Many Americans who witnessed the second strike will always remember thinking, "This is no accident, America is under attack!" As the terror mounted in Washington, D.C., and Pennsylvania, air defenders all over the country swung into action. The country was at war.

Out of a great American tragedy, comes a great American story, the epilogue yet to be written. On Sept. 11, heroic efforts were the order of the day both on the ground and in the air. Military commanders from the Air Force's "Total Force" and from all services ran to the sound of the guns — they were knocking down the Continental United States NORAD Region and air defense sector doors, willing to lend a hand. They came in the midst of war's fog and friction, amid the clamor and chaos of air attacks and reports of 21 additional hijackings that day. Against the backdrop of the second tower exploding again and again in replayed images on national television, they picked up telephones, wanting to know where to send their fighters. How many? How far? How soon?

At this writing, the United States continues to fight the war on terror around the world. The military heroes of Sept. 11 continue to serve in their vein of volunteerism, working hand in hand with CONR and the three air defense sectors: flying Combat Air Patrols, standing alert and doing whatever necessary to protect our vital interests. More than ever, the U.S. Air Force, Air National Guard, Air Force Reserve, U.S. Navy, U.S. Army, U.S. Customs, FBI, Federal Aviation Administration, and many more patriots are making America's skies safe and secure.

Since Sept. 11, the air sovereignty mission has grown tenfold and has evolved into a mission of full air defense. For months after the attacks, armed fighters, aerial tankers and airborne early warning aircraft flew Combat Air Patrols over American cities and national events — 24 hours a day, seven days a week. Aircraft radar detection and command and control capabilities have been radically improved throughout the country through the Herculean labors of the FAA, civilian contractors, airmen, and soldiers.

The mission has come full circle. Before the Sept. 11 tragedy, air sovereignty was viewed by some as a "sunset mission" — an unnecessary relic of the Cold War. It was hard to envision a nightmare where commercial airliners would be used as fuel-air bombs flown by homicidal pilots. Never before were airline hijackings within the United States considered a military responsibility; they were considered a criminal act and a law enforcement issue. Many things changed that day.

One thing that did not change was the dedication of the men and women assigned and attached to 1st Air Force and CONR. Their loyalty to the mission and sense of responsibility to the country never wavered, even when the mission was ignored, under-resourced and unpopular. As the air defense mission vaulted to the forefront of Department of Defense operations, a spirit of cooperation arose among military and federal agencies to keep our country's skies free.

Our lives and our world changed Sept. 11.
Air sovereignty changed Sept. 11.
This book will chronicle that story.

— **Retired Col.
William A. Scott,**
1st Air Force
director of plans,
programs and
requirements

*This book is dedicated to the
thousands of innocent people
who lost their lives
Sept. 11, 2001.
We will never forget you
or your loved ones you
left behind.*

White House photo by Paul Morse

*This book is for the
men and women
fighting the war on terror
in Operation Noble Eagle.*

Contents

ABOUT THE COVER: A Vermont Air National Guard F-16 assigned to the 158th Fighter Wing patrols the skies over New York City on Sept. 12, 2001. The photo was taken by Air Force Lt. Col. Terry Moultrup.

OPPOSITE PAGE: Firefighters unfurl the American flag at the Pentagon on Sept. 12, 2001.

CHAPTER 1

THE COLD WARRIORS:
Ready, alert and willing

America's air defense mission
changes with Soviet tide

The young airman at the Phoenix Air Defense Sector gazed at the radar screen in awe — there was nothing there. It was a surreal experience, "strange, really, watching all the planes disappearing from the scope," Bill Johnson remembers. "It was weird to come to work before midnight and just watch the scope gradually go blank. I was stationed at Luke Air Force Base, (Ariz.), at the time, looking all the way from California to New Mexico, and there wasn't anything in the sky."

It was the ultimate Cold War challenge: For 12 hours on Oct. 14, 1961, virtually all North American civilian aviation was halted so the U.S. Air Force could determine its air defense readiness. Air Defense Command's 41 interceptor squadrons, 25 Air National Guard squadrons and support aircraft from throughout the military — even the Royal Canadian Air Force — fought the simulated air war.

More than 1,000

fighter-interceptors were on full alert when the massive exercise began, and 400 Strategic Air Command bombers and tankers were deployed within 15 minutes to test the air defense ground environment. [1]

The North American Air Defense Command exercise — Sky Shield II — was an impressive display of America's air defense capabilities and the greatest war game of Johnson's 30-year career. "During peacetime air defense is very difficult, because you've got a lot of friendly people flying around," the retired Air Force chief master sergeant says. "During a 'war' it's easy, because you know who the good guys are. Sky Shield II was a great exercise, because we really got to fight."

But what really struck Johnson back then was the talk of Russian trawlers picked up by radar off the East and West coasts of the United States. "They weren't fishing boats, really, but they were out there," he recalls.

Spies or fishermen —

who's to say? But that autumn of 1961, there was the pervading sense that *the Reds were out there.* It was the Cold War, after all, and the Soviet threat scared the hell out of men, women and children from Topeka to Tupelo. America was facing its fears head-on, using the most sophisticated air defense system ever built to thwart a Soviet bomber attack. Sky Shield II proved the system fairly effective, especially at medium and high altitudes. But it also confirmed a weakness: the hostile, low-altitude bomber plane using electronic countermeasures to jam America's radars. [2]

Above: A flight crew from the 83rd Fighter Interceptor Squadron, Hamilton Air Force Base, Calif., scrambles to its F-101B "Voodoo" in 1961.

Left: A flight crew from the 27th Fighter Interceptor Squadron, March Air Force Base, Calif., scrambles to its F-86A "Sabrejets" in the spring of 1950.

THE COLD WARRIORS

"The threat was the bird with the red star."

— retired Air Force Col. Connie Mac Hostetler,
Cold War F-101 radar intercept officer

U.S. Air Force photo

Perched at the top of a 5,200-foot ridge southeast of Spokane in eastern Washington, Mica Peak Air Force Station definitely had four seasons, including rough winters which made crew changes difficult at times. The 823rd Radar Squadron operated the facility from 1955 through 1975. The facility continues to serve in the air defense role as a Joint Surveillance System site.

Some F-104A "Starfighter" pilots get a bird's-eye view of San Francisco's Golden Gate Bridge. The airplanes were assigned to the 83rd Fighter Interceptor Squadron, Hamilton Air Force Base, Calif., long since closed.

"The threat was the bird with the red star," says retired Air Force Col. Connie Mac Hostetler, an F-101 radar intercept officer at Dover Air Force Base, Del., in the early 1960s. "I was in the 98th Fighter Interceptor Squadron and there were squadrons like ours all over the country and we all did the same thing. We had aircraft on alert, slept in alert hangars — right at the end of the runway in most cases — and if an 'unknown' popped up in the airspace, we were scrambled. The controller would send us out to the unknown, we'd fly up alongside it, take a look and report back what we saw.

"We could be awakened in the middle of the night, 1 in the morning, it didn't make any difference. And we had to be airborne in five minutes."

Soviet bombers were indeed a high priority for the binational NORAD and its forces. As the fighting command, NORAD had many support organizations at its disposal: Canadian Air Command, the U.S. Air Force's ADC, Army Air Defense Command, and Naval Forces Continental Air Defense Command/NORAD. At the time of Sky Shield II, a quarter of a million Canadians and Americans were operating a multilayered and interlocking system of sites, control centers, manned interceptors, and surface-to-air missiles to defend against a potential bomber attack. [3]

New enemy, new war

Forty years later, and for the second time in American history, civilian aviation was halted again. But this war was real. Sept. 11, 2001, was the deadliest terrorist attack the country had ever seen. Hijackers transformed airliners into weapons of war that day, striking America's most revered symbols and murdering thousands of people in the grim process. A nation's heart was broken.

The military action was swift: Air National Guard fighters were immediately scrambled in a desperate attempt to take back America's skies. Amid the chaos, NORAD Commander Gen. Ralph E. Eberhart ordered a modified version of the Cold War plan SCATANA— Security Control of Air Traffic and Air Navigation Aids — to help the Federal Aviation Administration in its efforts to clear the skies. It was the first time it had happened since Sky Shield II.

A new enemy had emerged and spiraled out of control. Several years earlier America's air defense mission had become one of "air sovereignty" — the protection of America's air borders from terrorists, drug runners, rogue nations, and unknown threats. The Cold War was over and America's perception

One thing was constant before, during and after the Cold War: The mission was always focused outward.

AIR-2A Genie rocket aboard an F-101B

Photo courtesy of NORAD/USSPACECOM History Office

An airman inspects an AIR-2A "Genie" rocket on an F-101B "Voodoo." When the Voodoo entered service in 1957, it was the heaviest single-seat fighter the Air Force had seen.

of the Soviet bomber threat had changed dramatically.

Seven Air National Guard squadrons were dedicated to the NORAD (since renamed North American *Aerospace* Defense Command) air sovereignty mission before that tragic September morning; 14 fighter jets were on 24-hour alert, ready to fly when called upon. Airmen at the nation's three air defense sectors monitored the skies around the clock for any unknowns trying to enter sovereign American airspace.

The mission had changed: The last of the regular Air Force's fighter-interceptor squadrons — the 48th at Langley Air Force Base, Va., — had closed

in 1991, ADC was long gone, Cold War radar sites had for years been abandoned. A few thousand people — a far cry from air defense forces of the 1950s and 1960s — were performing NORAD's continental air sovereignty mission as members of 1st Air Force and the Continental United States NORAD Region.

"Our emphasis on the air defense role started fading with the meltdown of the Soviet Union," says retired Maj. Gen. Larry K. Arnold, 1st Air Force and CONR commander from December 1997 through July 2002. "However, we still maintained an air defense capability."[4]

One thing was constant before, during and after

the Cold War: The mission was always focused outward. "We always viewed an attack from within our borders as a law enforcement issue, not as an air defense issue," Arnold explains. "The reality is that any attack within the United States by any type of weapon has become an air defense issue." [5]

Cold War frenzy

In the four decades between Sky Shield II and SCATANA, America's air defense operations had seen many changes and challenges.

The Cold War frenzy began the summer of 1949 when America learned the Soviets had detonated an atomic bomb. The North Korean invasion of South Korea on June 25, 1950, only made matters worse. The Air Force, fearful of an all-out war with the Soviets, put its air defense forces on special alert. Major weaknesses were discovered, leading to the development of a new air defense command and control structure and Air Defense Identification Zones along the nation's frontiers. [6]

The U.S. Army Corps of Engineers was dispatched, and began building radar sites for America's new permanent air defense network. [7] By 1951, one of the first command and control stations was under construction at McChord Air Force Base, Wash. America's air defense mission was taking shape and the country was divided into 11 continental United States air defense regions. [8]

Searching for enemy planes wasn't left to the military alone — vigilance was the operative word for soldier and citizen alike. In 1952, the Air Force was actively recruiting for the Ground Observer Corps, civilian volunteers who would eye the skies for bombers penetrating American airspace.

In an era of McCarthyism and backyard bomb shelters, radio spots like this inspired 305,000 people to join: *"It may not be a very cheerful thought, but the Reds right now have about a thousand bombers that are quite capable of destroying at least 89 American cities in one*

raid. ... Won't you help protect your country, your town, your children? Call your local Civil Defense Office and join the Ground Observer Corps today." [9]

Air defense enthusiast Gene McManus was a member of the GOC unit "Hotel Kilo 25 Black" in the mid-1950s in Baltimore, Ohio.

"Back in those days, most of my friends and I were interested in the military and really wanted to be a part of it," McManus remembers. "I was in high school at the time ... we operated out of a small building with no facilities whatsoever, but it had windows you could take out and look through. If we heard an airplane, we'd rush out the door, find it in the air with our binoculars and try to identify it as best we could. We'd 'guesstimate' its altitude and heading and what kind of aircraft it was, and then we'd pick up the phone and call the operator at the filter center for an 'aircraft flash.' I think the whole thing was manned by high school kids. But we filled in the gaps until what became ADC radar sites were implemented."

The GOC performed its patriotic duty until its deactivation in early 1959 when short-range radars were deployed to detect low-flying airplanes.

As Hotel Kilo 25 Black searched for enemy bombers, an even scarier threat was emerging: the Soviet Intercontinental Ballistic Missile, or ICBM. America became painfully aware of this new danger on Oct. 4, 1957, when the Soviet Union launched Sputnik — man's first artificial satellite — into space. What frightened the most astute observer was how Sputnik was launched: by a ballistic missile that could carry a nuclear warhead. [10] With Sputnik came the realization that the enemy could possibly circumvent continental air defenses. [11]

The Soviet ICBM, heavy on the minds of the Cold Warriors, would ultimately change the nature of the mission. Not everyone agreed how the

Soviets would strike, but the Air Force believed an ICBM attack would be followed by waves of strategic bombers. [12] The bomber threat alone was very real, but many Congressmen thought money spent on bomber defense was wasted because of the overwhelming ICBM capability. Budget cuts to radar sites and the new Semiautomatic Ground Environment — SAGE — command and control program followed. [13]

Nevertheless, America's air defenses were mighty. In the late 1950s and early 1960s, nearly 100,000 people were assigned to ADC, the command that provided continental air defense resources for NORAD. [14] And several Air National Guard interceptor squadrons were participating successfully in the runway alert program. [15] By the end of 1961, NORAD controlled more than 100 fighter-interceptor squadrons, including some from the Canadian Forces; Boeing-Michigan Aeronautical Research Center, or "BOMARC," unmanned interceptor missiles; and "Nike" surface-to-air missiles. [16]

The SAGE network was completed that year and tied into 78 radar sites on the DEW (Distant Early Warning) Line, which stretched from Cape Lisburne, Alaska, to Cape Dyer, Canada. [17] The Mid-Canada Line, 1,000 miles south of the DEW Line, and the Pinetree Line on the American-Canadian border, bolstered the radar picture, potentially giving the countries a two- to three-hour warning of a bomber attack. [18] If the enemy was coming from either the Pacific or Atlantic, the Texas Tower radar platforms on the East Coast, Navy picket ships and dirigibles, and EC-121 early warning aircraft would act as offshore barriers. [19]

Two F-4 "Phantoms" intercept and escort a Soviet "Bear" bomber, the airplane that tested America's air defense force throughout the Cold War. The first of the Air Force's F-4s were delivered to Air Defense Command on May 27, 1963.

Wise SAGE system

Donald Bunce was a weapons controller at the Grand Forks Air Defense Sector, N.D., those booming years. His job entailed the four basic air defense functions: detect, identify, intercept, and destroy, "though we never really got to the last function," the retired Air Force colonel remembers. "We would monitor inbound aircraft from the north, northwest and northeast into our sector and before they got far, we'd identify them as friendly or unknown. If they were unknown, we'd scramble Grand Forks F-101s or F-89s from Fargo, (N.D.), to intercept. We did this by monitoring a radar scope, but SAGE was very new technology then. It was the first automated air defense system ... we had a lot of kinks to work out."

Photo courtesy of NORAD/USSPACECOM History Office

Johnson, too, remembers those early days. A few years before participating in Sky Shield II, his first Air Force assignment was to the SAGE test team in Massachusetts. It was 1955, and he and his fellow airmen were helping develop the AN/FSQ-7, a computer specifically designed for the air defense battle.

"The FSQ-7 actually became the first SAGE," Johnson says. "It did a great job, although it probably didn't have one 'meg' of RAM. But with SAGE you didn't have guys plotting airplanes on Plexiglas anymore. With that manual air defense system, you could only see about 200 miles from where you were located."

In the early 1950s, when airmen charted aircraft positions with a grease pencil, Ground Control

Intercept sites consisted of a search radar, height-finder radar and devices for communicating with interceptor pilots. [20] The high-tech SAGE would use radar and computers to paint a clear picture of the speed, location and direction of all planes in radar range. [21]

"In retrospect ... it was really a phenomenal experience helping put this thing together," Johnson says. "Most of us GIs were just GIs, we had an assignment and didn't see ourselves in the same vein as astronauts or anything. But now I realize we were involved in something that had a big impact on the country."

By 1962, after years of research and development, SAGE was operational at eight regional combat centers and 22 direction centers around the country. [22] Each SAGE combat center had many radar sites sending data to its respective SAGE direction center. The SAGE direction center sent the data to its respective air division. The Phoenix Air Defense Sector, for instance, sent its radar data to the 28th Air Division commander at Hamilton Air Force Base, Calif.

As modern and thorough as it was, the Air Force was well aware that SAGE blockhouses were vulnerable to Soviet ICBM attack. In the summer of 1961, even before SAGE was fully operational, NORAD planned for the Backup Interceptor Control system. Studies for an Airborne Warning and Control System were already underway. [23] The command's own control center at Ent Air Force Base, Colo., wouldn't stand up to Soviet attack any better than the SAGE blockhouse. Construction of the "rock" — 170,000 square feet of man-made caverns within Colorado's Cheyenne Mountain — began in 1961 and was completed by 1966. [24]

Ready to scramble

As the SAGE era progressed through the 1960s, hundreds of fighter pilots continued to guard America's skies from their alert shacks, scrambling to planes like Voodoos and Delta Darts at the first shrill tone of the alarm. Air Force bases dotted the landscape like diners on Route 66. Perrin Air Force Base, Texas; K.I. Sawyer Air Force Base, Mich.; Richards-Gebaur Air Force Base, Mo.; and Malmstrom Air Force Base, Mont.; were just a few ADC installations. Alert facilities were also found at many civil airports, from Atlantic City, N.J., to Walla Walla, Wash.

"There were so many bases in the interior of the country then," says retired Col. John D. Navin, former Vermont Air National Guard fighter-interceptor pilot. "And we had a number of fighter units across the northern tier, because it was popularly believed that a strike from the Soviet Union would come down over Canada. Early on, that's exactly what we were defending against — an attack over the poles."

When that unknown appeared and the alarm sounded, NORAD's fighter-interceptor pilots were ready, whether they encountered a lost civilian prop plane or a Soviet bomber off the coast of New England.

"Deterrence was the name of the game," says former fighter-interceptor pilot and retired Air Force Col. Harry Birkner. "We could not give someone the impression they could come over here and bomb us. That's what we wanted to portray, and that is what we did portray."

The training that pilots like Navin and Birkner received was intense and thorough. All-weather and instrument knowledge was crucial for air defense pilots who often flew their missions at night, when it would be easier for an unknown to enter American airspace.

That mission, in units like the 98th Fighter Interceptor Squadron, was written concisely to-the-point: *"To provide active Air Defense for the area assigned by achieving and maintaining a high level of Operational Readiness which will enable the unit to detect, intercept, identify, and/or destroy any unknown or unfriendly forces, under all conditions of weather, daylight or darkness."* [25]

Retired Air Force Col. Bill Stanfill remembers learning that very mission as a young lieutenant fresh out of flight school in 1966. "I entered Air Defense Command at Perrin Air Force Base, Sherman, Texas," he says. "It was the training base for ADC, and all ADC interceptor pilots went there first. We had six weeks of instrument training in the backseat of a T-33 under the hood. That made us all pretty darn good all-weather pilots.

"There were three interceptors then: the F-101, 102 and 106. Everyone trained on the F-102, then went on to their assignments from there."

Beyond the basics, the Air Force Interceptor Weapons School was the pinnacle of learning air defense for ground controller and flier alike. "I went twice to Interceptor Weapons School, once as a controller and once as a pilot," Birkner says. "It was one of the best schools for aviators I've ever been through. And for air defense, there was no better school and group of instructors anywhere. Controllers and pilots actually got to debrief the mission together, unlike in the real world where controllers are hundreds of miles away."

A former IWS commander, retired Air Force Col. Ron Stull, says the school "was the heart and soul of teaching air defense." Fourteen-hour training days were not uncommon, he says.

According to SabreJet Classics magazine, IWS instructors *"considered themselves to be the 'elite' of the all-weather interceptor business, as they were always ready to try something new and different. The instructors developed tactics to counter the electronic countermeasures*

NORAD'S FIGHTER FORCE

Through the years, NORAD has controlled the following approximate numbers of interceptor aircraft dedicated to its aerospace control mission, like this F-104A assigned to the 83rd Fighter Interceptor Squadron, Hamilton Air Force Base, Calif.

1958	5,800 *
1959	750
1976	325
1990	200
1997	175
2001	20 **

U.S. Air Force photo

*Includes approximately 3,600 reserve aircraft (2,200 active U.S. and Canadian aircraft); **denotes the normal compliment of alert fighters arrayed at 10 bases in the U.S. and Canada

SOURCE: NORAD PUBLIC AFFAIRS OFFICE

U.S. Air Force photo

In early 1970, 13 radar sites upgraded to Backup Interceptor Control capability under the BUIC III program, enabling them to function as mini Semiautomatic Ground Environment direction centers in the event of an attack on the main SAGE command and control facilities. The 637th Air Defense Group operated this BUIC III at Othello Air Force Station, Wash.

A formation of F-101 "Voodoos" assigned to the 15th Fighter Interceptor Squadron, Davis-Monthan Air Force Base, Ariz., flies through the clouds in this circa 1960 photo. Because of its weapons mix, speed and range, the Voodoo had no equal as an air defense interceptor.

anticipated by the Soviet bomber forces, perfected night firing on multiple target situations and regularly flew (illegally) in weather without an available alternate whenever their area of operations was socked in. The IWS instructors literally pushed the envelope of all-weather tactics to the limit (and beyond) of safety." [26]

"The Russians knew they could destroy us, but we also could destroy them."

— Dr. Rick Sturdevant,
deputy director,
Air Force Space Command History Office

Dying mission

Between the nation's highly trained air defense pilots and controllers — all using state-of-the-art equipment — America's ability to fend off an air attack remained strong. Air defense, however, was not the Air Force's top priority, and never was. It went back to the days of the Army Air Forces, when in the mid-1940s, air power projection advocates such as generals Carl A. Spaatz and Curtis LeMay saw delivery of the atomic bomb as the primary mission. [27] The idea of offensive air power as the best method of defense dominated Air Force thinking for years to come; air defense planners began fighting the budget battle. [28]

Years later, the fight was still on. In February 1966, Defense Secretary Robert McNamara put it this way to the House Subcommittee on Department of Defense Appropriations: "The elaborate defenses which we erected against the

Flight crews from the Texas Air National Guard 147th Fighter Interceptor Group sit alert in this circa 1960 photo. In August 1960 the unit began flying the F-102A fighter-interceptor to guard the Texas Gulf coast.

Photo courtesy of 147th Fighter Wing, Texas Air National Guard

Soviets' bomber threat during the 1960s no longer retain their original importance. Today, with no defense against the major threat, Soviet ICBMs, our anti-bomber defenses alone would contribute very little to our damage limiting objective ... for this reason we have been engaging in the past five years in a major restructuring of our defenses." [29]

McNamara was speaking at a tumultuous time for the United States military: the Vietnam War. A policy emerged during this era that had fateful consequences for air defense: "Mutual Assured Destruction," the idea that both superpowers would avoid war because a missile or bomber attack would lead to a devastating counterattack. [30]

"The MAD concept was employed to avoid nuclear war," explains Dr. Rick Sturdevant, deputy director of the Air Force Space Command History

Office. "The Russians knew they could destroy us, but we also could destroy them. Because each superpower had the capability to obliterate the other many times over, it would have been irrational to engage in direct, full-scale war. Mutual Assured Destruction, which often went by the less alarming euphemism 'nuclear deterrence,' was based on the belief that the Soviet Union would not be likely to launch a first strike if its leaders believed the U.S. would deliver an equally devastating retaliatory blow."

The era of MAD, the ICBM and Vietnam is characterized by many in the business as the end of the traditional air defense mission. "After Vietnam, air defense had really changed," Birkner says, who left the 48th Fighter Interceptor Squadron at Langley for Southeast Asia in 1970. "When there

Right: The U.S. Navy's Airship Airborne Early Warning Squadron One operated manned blimps that were an integral part of the contiguous NORAD radar barrier. The mission of the blimps was to provide warning of an air attack originating from over the North Atlantic in the late 1950s.

Below: The Texas Towers — three manned radar platforms operated in the late 1950s and early 1960s off the East Coast — served as a NORAD control and warning system of over-water attacks. Crews on the towers worked in a perilous environment; on Jan. 15, 1961, Texas Tower No. 4 was ripped apart during a fierce storm. None of the 28 people aboard — a caretaker crew there to renovate the structure that February — survived. The last of the towers, No. 3, was dismantled in March 1963.

Photos courtesy of Marty Isham

were multiple warheads on missiles, it made a little radar site sitting at the tip of Florida somewhere kind of insignificant, and we all accepted that as the mission drew down and went to the Guard."

As all eyes turned toward Vietnam, 13 regular Air Force fighter-interceptor squadrons closed their hangar doors. [31]

By 1971 there were 12 regular Air Force fighter-interceptor squadrons left in operation; three in the Canadian Forces; and 15 in the Air National Guard. [32] The Air Force ADC had been renamed *Aerospace* Defense Command, and the number of SAGE direction centers in the continental United States had been reduced to six. [33]

Retired Air Force Col. Connie Mac Hostetler witnessed the ever-changing mission from an excellent vantage: ADC headquarters in late 1972, upon his return from two tours in Vietnam. Working in the Chidlaw Building, downtown Colorado Springs, Colo., he was responsible for writing operating plans for all air defense units.

"During the time I was in Vietnam, a lot of ADC went over to the Guard units," he says. "Many of the fighter-interceptor assets went to the Guard and a lot of the fighter-interceptor squadrons folded. The perimeter air defense idea came in and a lot of the internal air defense squadrons closed down.

"The rationale was: 'Who is going to attack us from the inside? Who is going to attack Kansas City; Lockbourne (Air Force Base), Ohio; or Big Spring, Texas?' So as the restructuring of air defense began, everyone realized that the Guard

could do the same job as the active duty units and the active duty could be used for active duty needs."

"I think some people wondered about the Guard," he says. "But the Guard guys were sharp: their hangars were spotless, you could almost eat off the floor. Their aircraft were extremely good and their crews were good."

Says retired Air Force Maj. Jim Stumpf, a former F-101 radar intercept officer, 13th Fighter Interceptor Squadron, Glasgow Air Force Base, Mont.: "I got back from a tour in Vietnam and saw all these Guard units with 101s. As I kept watching this happen, the Guard units continued to do good work and take more and more of the mission."

◻◻◻

As America's air defense posture drew down, one thing remained unchanged: the Soviet threat. The U.S.S.R. continued to develop and refine its bomber defense, even after agreeing to an antiballistic missile treaty in 1972. [34] United States policy makers continued to believe a bomber defense was meaningless without a missile defense.

"It was clear to many people in the military, at least in their own minds, that the need for a robust air sovereignty fighter force structure was not necessary," says Navin, the former Vermont Guardsman and longtime air defense proponent.

"We didn't all necessarily share that opinion, but there were enough people in the Department of Defense — at the decision-making level — who didn't see it as necessary."

Air defense did get a shot in the arm in October 1971, when a Cuban airplane landed in New Orleans after flying undetected through American airspace. A congressional inquiry into the incident revealed that the 1,500-mile southern border between California and Florida had become virtually defenseless. In May 1972, Secretary of Defense Melvin R. Laird established the Southern Air Defense Network, which consisted of a reopened radar network along the Gulf Coast and alert fighter-interceptors at four bases. [35]

By sheer coincidence, the Louisiana Air National Guard 159th Tactical Fighter Group, based in New Orleans, had left the air defense business for a tactical role only months before the Cuban plane flew into the port city.

"It was a big surprise to everyone when that plane came in, but we were even more surprised that we were shutting down our alert mission," says Chief Master Sgt. Brian Krail, a Louisiana Air National Guardsman since 1966. "We were transitioning from F-102 fighter-interceptors to F-100s at the time of that incident. The F-100s we got were coming out of Vietnam, and they were outdated. The unit was changing. We had gone from a straight air defense mission throughout the 1960s to an air-to-ground tactical mission."

The Louisiana airmen had spent their Cold War days on alert with loaded F-102s ready to go at the end of the runway.

"We had, right on our ramp, two hangars with F-102s sitting there 24 hours a day, with pilots and crew, 365 days a year," Krail says. "We practiced mass loads and turnaround loads and all the procedures that go along with air defense. We would load everything we possibly could to get airborne to protect the country. Then we did turnaround loads when they'd come back from the mission, which meant we would refuel and reload the airplanes and get ready to launch for a second attack. All of a sudden we had F-100s on the ramp ... it was a shock to all of us."

The sun sets on Moriarty Air Force Station, N.M., — long since closed — which was home to the 768th Air Control and Warning Squadron.

Photo courtesy of Radomes, Inc., The Air Defense Radar Veterans' Association

Three F-106 "Delta Darts" assigned to the New Jersey Air National Guard soar through blue skies.

Two F-101B "Voodoos" from the 84th Fighter Interceptor Squadron, Hamilton Air Force Base, Calif., fly a training mission in 1967.

Peacetime protection

The mission was fading away. Vietnam was ending, and — in the military ranks anyway — talk was of MiG kills and combat, not continental air defense.

"All the heroes were those who fought the war in Vietnam," says retired Brig. Gen. John Broman, who spent most of his 34-year career in air defense at the 148th Fighter Wing, Minnesota Air National Guard.

"There is a tremendous society of brotherhood among fighter pilots, unequaled to anything I've ever seen. With air-to-air skills comes tremendous prestige. It's very difficult to compete with that.

"There's an old saying I find so true, that 'generals like to train to fight the last war,' so after Vietnam, we trained fighter-to-fighter," the former fighter-interceptor pilot says. "Then the radar environment deteriorated so badly, it almost made no sense to have interceptors. The air defense community had totally given up on the mission, it had been relegated to the Guard."

By 1976, 20 squadrons played an air defense role — 10 were from the Air National Guard. 36 Aerospace Defense Command — referred to as ADCOM by this time — was responsible for "peacetime protection of air sovereignty and early warning against bomber attack." 37

Only a few short years passed before ADCOM was disestablished — most of its assets absorbed into the Air Force Tactical Air Command. The new organization, Air Defense Tactical Air Command, or ADTAC, was established Oct. 1, 1979. 38 It was responsible for air defense under NORAD and reorganized as Headquarters 1st Air Force Dec. 6, 1985. 39

As America's air defense operations were downsizing and reorganizing, Russian "Bear" bombers were frequent fliers in North American airspace, flying off the Canadian and Alaskan and East coasts of the United States. America's air defenders — many flying F-15s and F-16s by then — were perfectly willing to "escort" them through. The Russians kept NORAD's 18 fighter-interceptor squadrons fairly busy. 40

"It's common knowledge that the Russians flew Tu-95 Bear aircraft off the East Coast of the United States on a fairly regular basis," says Lt. Col. Mark Stuart, a Soviet strategic systems analyst for 1st Air Force in the mid- to late-1980s. "It was a very busy time for air defense. We took the threat of aircraft penetrating United States airspace very seriously, because the Tu-95 is capable of carrying nuclear weapons. They were flying two-ships (a pair of airplanes) of those ... then they'd deploy

Right: A Soviet "Bear" bomber as photographed from an F-4E.

Opposite page: Two F-15 "Eagles" from the 48th Fighter Interceptor Squadron, Langley Air Force Base, Va., intercept a Bear in this circa 1985 photo.

Photo by Marvin Cox, courtesy of Marty Isham

Naval assets, the Bear 'D' and 'F' models, into Cuba. And they were all very capable aircraft at the time."

The Russians were proving a point, says Col. Chip Cumm, commander of the Massachusetts Air National Guard 102nd Fighter Wing alert detachment, Loring Air Force Base, Maine, in the late 1980s. "They wanted us to know they could do it and we wanted them to know we could get to them before they could hurt us," he says. "So our pilots picked them up way, way out over the water. Most of our intercepts were actually closer to Iceland than the United States."

"Those missions lasted five to eight hours, and we couldn't do it without a tanker for refueling," Cumm adds. "Once in awhile the AWACS (Airborne Warning and Control System aircraft) was there, but other times we just went out and found them on our own. With an F-15 radar against a Bear bomber, it's not as hard as it sounds. You can cover a lot of airspace with an F-15 radar against a bomber-size target at 30,000 feet. You can see them a long way away."

The camaraderie in the detachment — about 25 people — was unbelievable, Cumm says. Like family. And like so many other air defense units before it, it would cease to exist. It was 1993. The Soviet Union was no more. The Berlin Wall had fallen. All regular Air Force fighter-interceptor squadrons had deactivated.

The Cold War was over.

But the professionalism and pride in the mission

would never die.

"Even after it was announced the unit would shut down, we had a no-notice NORAD alert force evaluation and got the first 'Outstanding' rating given to an alert detachment — and that was an Outstanding across the board," Cumm says. "Our people were so good, they could teach the inspectors how to do the business. Nobody did it better."

And when all that went away, "It was horrible ... gut-wrenching to see it close.

"It was the best job I ever had."

1 Air Defense Command, *History of the Air Defense Command: July - December 1961* (Ent Air Force Base, Colo.), 295-298.

2 Ibid., 299.

3 Thomas Fuller, "NORAD at 40: Historical Overview" (North American Aerospace Defense Command History Office, 1997), n.p.

4 Eric Hehs, "Major General Larry Arnold, Commander, 1st Air Force, Tyndall Air Force Base, Florida," *Code One, Lockheed Martin Aeronautics Company*, First Quarter 2002, 4.

5 Ibid., 4.

6 David F. Winkler, *Searching the Skies: The Legacy of the United States Cold War Defense Radar Program* (Langley Air Force Base, Va.: United States Air Force Air Combat Command, 1997), 22.

7 Ibid., 22.

8 United States Air Force Air Combat Command, *Cold War Infrastructure for Air Defense: The Fighter and Command Missions* (Langley Air Force Base, Va.: United States Air Force Air Combat Command, 1999), 9.

9 Kenneth Schaffel, *The Emerging Shield: The Air Force and the Evolution of Continental Air Defense, 1945-1960* (Washington, D.C.: Office of Air Force History, United States Air Force, 1991),

158-159.

10 Ibid., 255.

11 Winkler, *Searching the Skies,* 37.

12 Schaffel, *The Emerging Shield*, 261.

13 Winkler, *Searching the Skies,* 39.

14 Schaffel, *The Emerging Shield,* 286.

15 Charles J. Gross, *Prelude to the Total Force: The Air National Guard, 1943-1969* (Washington, D.C.: Office of Air Force History, United States Air Force, 1985), 125.

16 Schaffel, *The Emerging Shield,* 268.

17 Ibid., 215, 268.

18 Fuller, "NORAD at 40: Historical Overview," n.p.

19 Fuller, "NORAD at 40: Historical Overview," n.p.; Schaffel, *The Emerging Shield,* 268.

20 Schaffel, *The Emerging Shield,* 204.

21 Ibid., 204.

22 Winkler, *Searching the Skies,* 41.

23 Ibid., 41-44.

24 Ibid., 45.

25 Ted R. Sturm, "Voodoos," *The Airman*, n.d., 12.

26 Larry Davis, "Interceptor Weapons School," *SabreJet Classics,* Summer 2000, n.p.

27 Winkler, *Searching the Skies,* 15.

28 Ibid., 15.

29 Ibid., 37.

30 Schaffel, *The Emerging Shield*, 268.

31 Air Force Space Command, *NORAD Dedicated Interceptor Squadrons, 1957-85*, n.p., n.d., Doc. SDI-54A.

32 Ibid., n.p.

33 Winkler, *Searching the Skies,* 47.

34 Schaffel, *The Emerging Shield,* 272.

35 Ibid., 272.

36 *NORAD Dedicated Interceptor Squadrons, 1957-85,* n.d., n.p.

37 Winkler, *Searching the Skies,* 48.

38 Paul E. McAllister, *TAC Strategic Air Defense Reference Book: October 1979-December 1989* (Langley Air Force Base, Va.: Headquarters 1st Air Force, 1990), 4.

39 Ibid., 13.

40 *NORAD Dedicated Interceptor Squadrons, 1957-85.*

Four F-106A "Delta Darts" assigned to the 318th Fighter Interceptor Squadron, McChord Air Force Base, Wash., fly over Mount Rainier. The F-106 was similar in appearance to the F-102 with its delta-shaped wing and no tail plane, but had many improvements, most notably, speed. The 177th Fighter Wing, New Jersey Air National Guard, was the last unit to fly the aircraft in an operational role.

U.S. Air Force photo

NEW ERA, NEW STRUGGLES:
Surviving the post-Cold War

CHAPTER 2

Air National Guard protects America's air borders
from the frightening, wily unknown

An F-16 assigned to the North Dakota Air National Guard 119th Fighter Wing breaks from a fellow "Happy Hooligan" in blue November skies.

It was an unusually cold Virginia afternoon, Dec. 6, 1985, the day 1st Air Force reactivated for the third time in history. A precise fingertip formation of four F-15 "Eagles" soared over Langley Air Force Base at the ceremony to celebrate the occasion. As the deafening roar of the jet fighters filled the winter air, Maj. Gen. Buford D. Lary couldn't help but be proud: it was a perfect fly-by and the pilots above were his own, members of the 48th Fighter Interceptor Squadron and part of his new command. First Air Force was taking responsibility for America's air sovereignty and Lary

was becoming the leader of a more focused and — in his words — "cleaner" organization.

First Air Force was replacing Air Defense Tactical Air Command, a staff organization that had lived a strange, confusing existence since 1979. "Nobody even knew what ADTAC was," admits one insider. Although part of Tactical Air Command headquarters and technically in charge of TAC air defense forces, ADTAC was separate from TAC in both structure and operation and never really accepted into TAC's inner sanctum. [1] There was even a nickname for air defenders back then:

"Coneheads." Just like the "Saturday Night Live" characters that share their name, the ADTAC folks were the weird neighbors next door. [2]

The rebirth of 1st Air Force was good for the mission, Lary says. "Morale went up," the retired lieutenant general recalls. "We were now a command that had a peacetime role, a warfighting role, a command and control system right there at Langley, and our own command post. And we had some well-qualified people to do all this."

The warfighting role was accomplished with the creation of the Continental United States North American Aerospace Defense Command Region — CONR — in February 1986. [3] This ensured air sovereignty remained under NORAD direction; the CONR command structure would parallel that of the Alaskan and Canadian NORAD regions. "I was commander of 1st Air Force in peacetime and commander of the Continental NORAD Region in wartime," Lary says. "You never are one or the other, you are sort of both, but become beholden to the commander in chief of NORAD in the warfighting role and the commander of TAC in peacetime."

Air sovereignty had found its niche: Lary had direct lines of communication with NORAD's four continental air division commanders; the commanders, each with their own geographical area to protect, could launch fighter jets at a moment's notice. Command and control technicians at the nation's air defense sectors were eyeing radar scopes for any "unknowns" approaching the borders. They were all working together under the prestige of a numbered air force, the "senior warfighting echelon of the United States Air Force." [4] But the years ahead would be challenging as old threats died and new threats emerged.

A pilot from the 120th Fighter Wing, Montana Air National Guard, prepares to lower the canopy of an F-16C prior to leaving on a training mission.

That old threat kept 1st Air Force busy during Lary's tenure and was alive and well when he relinquished command to Maj. Gen. Jimmie V. Adams in July 1987.

"The Soviet 'Bear' bomber was the major threat we faced in sizable numbers, even then," says retired Gen. Adams. "We were quite busy contending with active scrambles for that intrusion into our sovereign airspace."

The Soviets deployed bombers to Cuba throughout the 1980s, flying too close to the United States for NORAD comfort. The cat-and-mouse game at 30,000 feet was a nuisance the Air Force

could handle, but what about the new threat on the horizon? The fast and low-flying Soviet cruise missile could evade radar coverage and presented a new challenge for America's air sovereignty team.

"There was an evolving cruise missile threat associated with the bombers and growing concern about the manned bomber and cruise missile nuclear threat," Adams explains. "And the capability we had against cruise missiles was limited. It is a very small target and very difficult to detect on radar, so I was much more comfortable dealing with the bomber threat."

The American-Canadian partnership at NORAD worked to modernize the aging air defense system and improve the radar coverage the entire mission relied upon. By the late 1980s the North Warning System was under construction to replace the Distant Early Warning Line arctic radar chain, but wouldn't achieve initial capability until 1995. [5] The newly created United States Space Command, meanwhile, was charged with providing NORAD missile warning and space surveillance capability. [6]

But North America's strongest line of defense remained its most basic: 52 armed F-106s, F-15s and F-16s operated by both the regular Air Force and Air National Guard. A 1974 Department of Defense study had concluded that two fighters each on continuous alert at 26 sites was adequate to maintain peacetime air sovereignty — a standard that continued through the late 1980s. [7]

Mission impossible?

Despite modernization attempts and the relatively healthy fighter force, a crucial part of America's air defense structure was lost in the 1980s, says retired Brig. Gen. John Broman, former commander of the 148th Fighter Wing, Minnesota Air National Guard. Between 1986 and 1988, 17 of 24 radar sites on the Pinetree Line on the U.S.-Canadian border were closed. [8] Combined with the subsequent elimination of Canada's Air Defense Identification Zone —
ADIZ — air defense on the northern tier was becoming "mission impossible," Broman says. With no ADIZ, all flights originating in Canada and crossing the U.S. border were presumed "friendly by origin." [9]

"When the radar sites closed down, there was a particularly interesting lack of capability," Broman explains. "Eventually there was also no radar coverage along the

Photo by Master Sgt. Don Taggart, 177th Fighter Wing, New Jersey Air National Guard

west coast of Canada. An airplane with enough range could enter Canada from the west and then just turn south to fly over the United States at any altitude below positive controlled airspace without any risk of detection by any air defense radar or any interest by Federal Aviation Administration radar."

For years fighter pilots had sat alert at places like Selfridge Air National Guard Base, Mich.; Niagara Falls International Airport, N.Y.; and Hector Field, N.D. But with no way to identify an airborne threat, or "unknown rider," their very existence was called into question.

As 1st Air Force commander, Adams was faced with a dilemma. In 1988 he recommended NORAD close six alert sites near the U.S.-Canadian border — sites operated by the Air National Guard. [10] "Once we took away the Pinetree Line and ADIZ, I had no way of picking up those unknowns because they were friendly by definition, and that was agreed to by the U.S. and Canadian governments as a way to pay for modernizing the DEW Line," Adams says. "The question I had when I came aboard was: 'If I can't identify these guys as unknowns, why would I want airplanes on alert to go intercept them?' I had no procedures and no radar in place and no capability to exercise an ADIZ. ... It made no sense to spend all this money on 24-hour-a-day alert. But I was a little naïve about the powers of the Air National Guard, and naïve that it was 50 jobs per alert site. ... I created a real fire storm."

The idea didn't materialize right away, but was a sign of things to come. Peripheral defense — fighter-interceptors at strategic locations on the rim of the continental United States — was the wave of the future.

By 1990 the Department of Defense called for eventual closure of the northern tier alert sites. [11] American and Canadian fighters, in smaller numbers but formidable foes nonetheless, were providing North America's air sovereignty: protection from drug-smuggling aircraft and other unknown airborne threats. But the glory days of air defense — when hundreds of NORAD fighters were ready to intercept and destroy fleets of Soviet bombers — were over.

Above: Staff Sgt. Timothy M. Jacobs, a tracking technician at the Southeast Air Defense Sector, Tyndall Air Force Base, Fla., keeps an eye on the Gulf of Mexico for airborne threats to the United States. The command and control aspect of the air sovereignty mission became an Air National Guard responsibility in the late 1990s.

Left: An F-16 from the New Jersey Air National Guard 177th Fighter Wing darts through blue skies, as seen through the canopy of the jet beneath it.

Photo courtesy of 148th Fighter Wing, Minnesota Air National

Fit for a militia

As the Soviet Union crumbled and the decade gave way to overseas operations like Desert Storm and Joint Endeavor, air defense requirements continued to change. America wasn't so worried about Soviet bombers anymore and an attack on U.S. soil seemed unlikely. Money was tight and the Air Force was downsizing and reorganizing. In the early 1990s the Air Force consolidated from 13 to eight major commands and inactivated many proud wings and squadrons; by 1998 it would cut

its 600,000-plus personnel almost in half. [12] As early as 1990, senior leaders were exploring ways to spare the air sovereignty mission from the budget ax. [13]

A smaller 1st Air Force staff moved its headquarters to Tyndall Air Force Base, Fla., in late 1991. All air divisions had inactivated and the continental United States was divided into four air defense sectors. Several 1st Air Force duties had been reassigned elsewhere. By the end of the year, the 48th Fighter Interceptor Squadron — the last regular Air Force squadron of its kind — inactivated, leaving air defense flying to 11 Air

National Guard fighter wings. [14]

With all air defense flying in Air Guard hands, it seemed natural to many that air defense sector operations — the command and control aspect of the mission involving aircraft surveillance and identification— also reside there.

A lead supporter of the idea was Air Force Chief of Staff Gen. Merrill A. McPeak. "The Air Guard had been performing the mission for many years," says the retired general. "They understood it well. ... Why should they not command the numbered air force that stood at the top of this activity?" [15]

□□□

Former Air National Guard director, retired Maj. Gen. Donald Shepperd, says McPeak's proposal was right on target. "General McPeak felt the Air National Guard had been the guardian of air defense for years and therefore command and control of the mission belonged with the Guard," Shepperd says. "He also saw great force structure and money problems coming and thought if you put air defense in the Guard it becomes a Guard responsibility. It was one more fight he didn't have to fight."

Saving the mission was paramount, Shepperd believes. "The transition of 1st Air Force was about preserving some type of infrastructure simply because it did not seem wise to leave our air borders open. ... At that point it wasn't about a Soviet attack, but about our air borders and our air sovereignty."

By 1994, Air National Guard Maj. Gen. Philip G. Killey was in command of the federal mission — unheard of for a militiaman. His organization would become a strange hybrid: subordinate to NORAD, part Air Combat Command (formerly TAC), part National Guard Bureau, and misunderstood by many.

Killey, a South Dakotan and longtime fighter pilot, was to reorganize the entire numbered air force — about 1,300 people — from a regular Air

"The transition of 1st Air Force was about preserving some type of infrastructure simply because it did not seem wise to leave our air borders open. ... At that point it wasn't about a Soviet attack, but about our air borders and our air sovereignty."

— Retired Maj. Gen. Donald Shepperd, former Air National Guard director

Two F-16s assigned to the Minnesota Air National Guard 148th Fighter Wing, Duluth, fly across blue skies and light clouds. The 148th operates a 24-hour alert facility at Tyndall Air Force Base, Fla.

Force to Air National Guard organization in less than three years. [16]

The Air National Guard fighter wings of 1st Air Force wouldn't be affected. But the airmen at the Northeast, Southeast and Western air defense sectors; the headquarters staff; and two support squadrons; all had to be handled individually. A 1st Air Force transition team was formed to keep the evolving air sovereignty mission going as regular Air Force members were replaced by Guardsmen.

□□□

Retired Col. John D. Navin was Killey's right-hand man during the conversion. He emphasizes that the mission was foremost in their minds as they worked to take care of people first.

"We had to keep our people in focus as we turned an entire numbered air force over to Air National Guard command and control," the former Vermont Air National Guardsman says. "Even back then we kept an eye on Soviet long-range aviation capability, and no, didn't envision a wave of bombers coming over the poles like people thought in the 1950s and 1960s. However, we still believed the capability was there, maybe not the intent, but the capability. And we needed to have a capability to thwart that. The newer threat emerging was the rogue actor, the nation-state that had the capability and intent to use cruise missiles. We kept our eye on that threat as we made this transition."

Yes the Cold War was over, but "bottom line, air sovereignty means we need to know who's flying in our airspace," Killey said in a post-transition interview.

"We can't afford to have our skies, our borders of our airspace, wide open to whoever wants to fly in. We need to know what that traffic is. And we need to have a system of identifying unknown aircraft." [17]

Overshadowed by doubt

As Air Guard members joined 1st Air Force in the mid-to late-1990s, many signed waivers acknowledging their job would end if and when the mission did. Job security was no guarantee given the circumstances. [18]

Historically, the mission had seen its share of struggles. "Air Force strategy through the years was one of forward engagement overseas," explains retired Col. William A. Scott, a former 1st Air Force vice commander with 30 years' Air Force experience in both air defense and tactical operations. "Back in the 1950s, '60s and '70s, the Air Force world was split into two commands. Tactical Air Command fought wars 'over there,' and Aerospace Defense Command fought wars 'over here.' When ADCOM merged with TAC in 1979, the mission submerged into the 'over there' crowd who had little time and little patience for homeland defense."

Was the transition of 1st Air Force even necessary? "There were people who did not believe there was any need for the transition of 1st Air Force and CONR simply because they did not see a need for the mission, period," Navin says.

Some believed air sovereignty was robbing from other areas in a time of Air Force-wide cutbacks, he says. Even some in the Air National Guard were reluctant to see money dedicated to homeland air defense, Navin concedes. "People did not see a need for that kind of Air National Guard manpower

> *"The newer threat emerging was the rogue actor, the nation-state that had the capability and intent to use cruise missiles."*
>
> **— Retired Col. John D. Navin, 1st Air Force adviser**

Florida Air National Guard photo by retired Lt. Col. Chris N. Michalakis

Photo courtesy of 177th Fighter Wing, New Jersey Air National Guard

Above: An F-16 from the Florida Air National Guard 125th Fighter Interceptor Group escorts a Russian "Bear" bomber off the Florida coast in this Cold War-era photo. The 125th began flying F-15s in 1995 and was redesignated a fighter wing.

Left: The Cold War barely over, a New Jersey Air National Guard F-16 assigned to the 177th Fighter Group — now the 177th Fighter Wing — escorts a Russian MiG-29 to and from an air show in the early 1990s.

NEW ERA, NEW STRUGGLES

in air defense," he says. "People thought it was an absolute waste to put that manpower into a mission area that would totally go away anyway."

In the early post-Cold War years, the military at large believed the air defense threat nonexistent, Scott says. "There were many people in both the Air National Guard and active duty Air Force who didn't believe in the mission," says the former commandant of the Air Force's Squadron Officer School. "The threat at the time was perceived as nil.

"The vast majority of the hurdles 1st Air Force and CONR faced were at the mid-management staff level of colonels and below. The one common thread of responsibility could be found at the highest levels — once given the specific responsibility of air defense and air sovereignty through their positions as commander in chief of NORAD or Air Combat Command, they wouldn't let the mission die."

Staff Sgt. Sarah Davis gathers information on an unknown aircraft while "on scope" at the Western Air Defense Sector, McChord Air Force Base, Wash.

Washington Air National Guard photo by Master Sgt. Randy La Brune

An Oregon Air National Guard member from the 142nd Fighter Wing prepares an F-15 "Eagle" for flight.

But Scott says the mission remained underfunded and unpopular. A monumental challenge for Navin, Killey and the transition staff was proving to doubting military minds that 1st Air Force was a legitimate organization performing a legitimate mission.

"Major General Killey and I spent more time in the Pentagon trying to convince general officers that the mission was not only viable, but absolutely necessary, than I care to think about," Navin says. "Every single time, you'd walk away from there with that horrible feeling in the pit of your stomach and think, 'We're fighting a losing battle.'"

Shepperd says Air Force leaders may have lost interest in air defense. "We've seen this many times," he says. "When a mission is shed to the Guard, the Guard has to really fight for advocacy because there's none left in the Air Force and that has implications for ... funding and political advocacy."

☐☐☐

Although the transition wasn't easy and not everyone agreed necessary, Killey believes it was the perfect example of the Total Force concept — the unified powers of the Air Force, Air National Guard and Air Force Reserve. [19] The Air National Guard was relieving the Air Force of an important task as airmen were deploying far and wide and doing much more with much less. The Air Force didn't have time for the non-war at home; the Gulf War and monitoring no-fly zones in Southwest Asia was much hotter.

Air sovereignty would live by default, Scott says: "Most of what people talked about back then wasn't military action, but the threat of embarrassment to the United States. We didn't think Cuban MiGs would attack us, but they'd embarrass us. That potential for political embarrassment was a problem for us and NORAD."

The reality through the growing pains was the mission itself. Right during the transition, a highly publicized incident reminded people why they were there in the first place.

On Feb. 24, 1996, two Brothers to the Rescue aircraft flew near Cuban airspace and were shot down by Cuban MiG fighter jets. Four people from the Miami-based exile organization were killed.

"First Air Force had the only around-the-clock command and operation centers capable of responding with Combat Air Patrols," Killey said in a 1998 interview. "Our quick and certain response not only proved that we are an indispensable member of the aerospace defense team, but that America was serious about its air sovereignty." [20]

That winter day was a lively one at Tyndall's Southeast Air Defense Sector. Command and control technicians scrambled F-16s from the alert detachment of the 148th Fighter Wing, Minnesota Air National Guard. In only a few minutes, the pilots were over the blue Gulf waters assisting in the search-and-rescue operation. From monitoring radar scopes to launching airplanes, everyone did exactly what they were trained to do that day: protect America's air borders. [21]

> "There was always a movement afoot to further shut down 1st Air Force, CONR and the NORAD mission in general to the point that I always thought I might be out of there."
>
> — Retired Maj. Gen. Larry K. Arnold, former 1st Air Force commander

The transition of 1st Air Force to Air National Guard command and control was nearly complete. Critical thinkers in headquarters briefing rooms were discussing the new threat on the horizon. Lurking in the shadows was a dangerous underworld of airborne drug-runners, terrorists and rogue nations with frightening capabilities.

"By about 1995, even before the Brothers to the Rescue incident, people at 1st Air Force were talking about things like the rogue actors, the nation-states that had the capability and intent to use cruise missiles," Navin says. "We didn't use the word 'asymmetric' but began talking about terrorism."

"And by 1998, many people were talking about 1st Air Force and doing away with the sectors and said we didn't need the mission," he continues. "That was only two years after the shoot-down of Brothers to the Rescue by the Cuban MiGs. Things fade into the recesses of peoples' minds rather rapidly."

Mission at risk

In December 1997, Maj. Gen. Larry K. Arnold assumed command of 1st Air Force, CONR and a dying mission. Earlier that year, the Department of Defense had released "The Report of the Quadrennial Defense Review." The QDR outlined the conversion of six continental air defense squadrons to general purpose, training or other missions. [22] This "four-corners defense" idea called for alert sites at Cape Cod, Mass.; Homestead, Fla.; Riverside, Calif.; and Portland, Ore. [23] The other six squadrons in 1st Air Force, as suggested in the QDR, would convert to a multirole mission.

Left: American and Canadian forces work together to accomplish the binational NORAD mission, monitoring the scopes at the Western Air Defense Sector, McChord Air Force Base, Wash.

Below: Maj. John Larson, an F-16 pilot with the 119th Fighter Wing, North Dakota Air National Guard, completes a mission.

Washington Air National Guard photo by Tech. Sgt. Randy LaBrune

Photo by Master Sgt. William Quinn, 119th Fighter Wing, North Dakota Air National Guard

"When I first moved down to Tyndall as vice commander of 1st Air Force, the QDR had just been released," Arnold, since retired, says. "I moved to Tyndall and thought, 'well here I am in Florida, I ought to think about buying a boat.' And I never bought a boat because there was always a movement afoot to further shut down 1st Air Force, CONR and the NORAD mission in general to the point that I always thought I might be out of there. So I never bought a boat the whole time I was there.

"The QDR didn't make any sense at all," Arnold continues. "Four-corners defense might be good for basketball, and that's where the term comes from ... but it had absolutely no applicability to defending our country. It was ridiculous yet it became popular. So there was a fight just to maintain the number of alert sites that we had. We felt we could operate fairly reasonably with about 10 sites and thought eight was the absolute highest risk we could take. We ended up with seven. I didn't feel particularly comfortable with seven because there are great large distances between the alert sites."

The four-corners proposal was met with resistance from NORAD Commander in Chief Gen. Howell M. Estes III, who wrote to the Joint Chiefs of Staff that a minimum of seven alert sites were needed to maintain the nation's air sovereignty.

In the end, Estes won the battle and alert sites were added at Hampton, Va.; Panama City, Fla.; and Houston, Texas; where all three multirole squadrons would support air sovereignty. [24] But Arnold believes the real issue was the move to close 1st Air Force completely "without any alternative way of doing the mission." There was also pressure to close other numbered air forces, Arnold says, as Air Force leaders searched for better ways to fight wars, which is traditionally through numbered air forces.

As the QDR furor died down, the move to close 1st Air Force did not. By the summer of 1998, Air Combat Command, as the CONR force provider, would search for ways to organize its forces amid

Photo courtesy of 147th Fighter Wing, Texas Air National Guard

In the Internet age, pride in the air sovereignty mission is displayed on the tail of an F-16 assigned to the 147th Fighter Wing, Texas Air National Guard.

personnel shortages and an increased operations tempo. "I got a call from General (Richard) Hawley, who was the commander of ACC, and he said: 'My staff has given me a compelling argument as to why we should move all the forces out of 1st Air Force and move them into 8th, 9th and 12th air forces,'" Arnold recalls. "And he allowed me to respond to him. And when I did respond, he left all 10 units in 1st Air Force."

In another phone call between the two generals, Hawley reiterated to Arnold that the ACC staff was still considering ways to reorganize its numbered air forces. "General Hawley gave them a very short answer that was exactly the right answer," Arnold says. "It was really a question. He said to his staff: 'I have no position on whether we close 1st Air Force or not, but is there a better way to do the mission?'

"And that stumped them. I think they thought there was no mission, but as a four-star general, he realized we had to protect our borders. That question alone: 'Is there a better way to do the mission?' put to bed the idea of closing 1st Air Force, at least for awhile."

❑❑❑

Hawley says his command was faced with the challenge of best organizing its fighter force at a time of frequent deployments and a serious pilot shortage. "We were trying to figure out how to relieve the personnel tempo of people who were being pulled hither and yond to go cope with Northern Watch and so forth," the retired general says. "(The command needed) more general purpose fighters in the fighter rotation to support the overseas commitments and therefore spread the workload more evenly. ... Most of the 1st Air Force units were specialized solely in air defense, and in our rotations we needed people with a specialty in air superiority and dropping bombs."

"We had two problems," Hawley continues. "We had a lot of numbered air forces and not enough people to man them. The other problem was the operations tempo and personnel tempo and how to get the Air Force organized in a way that we could rotate forces in and out of the fights we had to man on a more rational basis ... to give people some predictability in their lives.

"The air defense issue was one of figuring out a way to absorb the air defense squadrons into the general purpose force structure so that we could use them ... and where that idea fell apart was, 'How do you do this and get the air defense mission accomplished?' "

Although the idea fizzled at Air Combat Command, Hawley says air sovereignty still remained a low Air Force priority. "Many people in the Air Force thought it was a waste of money and time to maintain a dedicated air defense force and the reason is not many people had thought about the basic, national responsibility to maintain sovereignty over our airspace, whether there's a threat to it or not," he says. "Among those who had given it some thought, air sovereignty was important."

A better way?

When the National Guard Bureau began studying 1st Air Force's closure in 1999, Arnold took action. [25] He didn't think there was a better way to provide air sovereignty, but he wanted to prove that to himself and others. He looked toward written doctrine — the Bible of all things Air Force — and says he believed the organization was operating "in a very sound way." But Arnold wanted the issue examined. *Was there a better way to provide continental air sovereignty?*

"I wanted a study before the next QDR that said, 'Here's how we do the mission now, here's alternative ways we can do the mission,' " Arnold explains. "If there was a better way that was doctrinally sound, I was prepared to beat the drums and go do that."

"I wanted a team to talk to the commanders of NORAD and ACC and the leadership all over the Air Force and find out for me, find out if there's no mission," Arnold says. "And I said, 'If there's no mission, we'll shut down now.' "

With the backing of Air National Guard director Maj. Gen. Paul A. Weaver Jr., Arnold asked Maj. Gen. Paul Pochmara, a Michigan Air National Guardsman, to form a "Roles and Missions" team. Pochmara was the Air National Guard assistant to Air Force Materiel Command at the time and former commander of the 113th Tactical Fighter Wing,

District of Columbia Air National Guard.

"I was from outside the air defense world," Pochmara, since retired, says. "I flew fighters all my life and when Larry Arnold and Paul Weaver wanted someone to do the study, they wanted someone experienced in fighters with knowledge of air defense, but not a card-carrying air defender. I have sat air defense alert in Japan, but I was never a 1st Air Force-type of person and had never sat alert in the United States. ... I was close enough to the mission to have credibility but far enough away

1999, visiting other numbered air forces, NORAD, the National Guard Bureau, and Air Combat Command to find answers to the questions that kept Arnold guessing. The team was armed with a one-hour presentation that outlined the military's responsibility for protecting the nation's air sovereignty and supported its case with excerpts from the U.S. Constitution, Department of Defense policy and ACC directives.

"Universally, except for going up to NORAD, I think when we walked in the door we were

Photo by Eric Hehs,
Code One magazine

An F-16 from the Vermont Air National Guard 158th Fighter Wing takes off.

to have credibility. I would not be preaching to the choir."

Pochmara says he initially questioned the need for the study and wouldn't allow himself to be swayed by opinions on either side. "When we put together the team, 1st Air Force wanted me to be an honest broker and I was told to say it like it is," he says. "When I chose the members of this team, I chose some who did not see a need for air defense, some like myself who just didn't know and some from the 1st Air Force staff who were very zealous in their beliefs. ... I assembled people on this team who could balance each other out."

The 12-member "RAM" team set out in late

perceived with neither reticence nor support," Pochmara says. "They weren't necessarily hostile or against us, but we did not walk into friendly audiences either."

Maj. Gen. Mike Haugen, adjutant general of the North Dakota National Guard and RAM team member, says the group discussed everything from technology to the future of the air sovereignty mission to the terrorist threat. "We made some pretty bold predictions in our briefing," he says. "In fact, it included a photo of Osama bin Laden as the world's most dangerous terrorist. ... We didn't predict how the terrorists would strike but predicted they would strike."

Pochmara says the team wanted to convey the definition of air sovereignty. He puts it into basic terms. "You have your house in your neighborhood and you don't want anyone to break into it," he says. "But anyone, at will, can break into your house when you're not there or when you are there. And you can't really stop them. Do you leave your door open, do you unlock your doors because you can't stop somebody?

"We're not going to do that as a nation; we're going to make some attempt to keep our doors locked and protect ourselves and that's what sovereignty means."

In the end of their year together, the RAM team wrote a report concluding, "there are no better ways, just other ways," to perform the mission. Air sovereignty, the team found, is a valid and necessary military responsibility. Team leader Pochmara found himself a bigger supporter of the mission than he'd realized and the hesitant audiences gained new perspectives. "The overall consensus from people was: 'I understand 1st Air Force is valuable and needs to continue doing the work it does,'" Pochmara says.

Threat of the day

As the RAM team was examining the need for continental air sovereignty, a comprehensive look at America's future was well underway at the highest levels. The United States Commission on National Security/21st Century, led by former Sens. Gary Hart and Warren B. Rudman, released its first of three reports in September 1999. "New World Coming: American Security in the 21st Century," stated that *"America will become increasingly vulnerable to hostile attack on our homeland, and our military superiority will not entirely protect us."* [26]

"We should expect conflicts in which adversaries, because of cultural affinities different from our own, will resort to forms and

> *"We made some bold predictions in our briefing. In fact, it included a photo of Osama bin Laden as the world's most dangerous terrorist."*
>
> — Maj. Gen. Mike Haugen,
> adjutant general,
> North Dakota National Guard

levels of violence shocking to our sensibilities," reads an excerpt from the report. [27]

Discussions of new threats were everywhere, Scott says, yet the move to kill air sovereignty remained. "At about the same time this was all happening, there was an emerging debate within military academic circles about the asymmetric threat to the United States," Scott says. "A number of papers were published as we were struggling to stay alive. People did studies, including the Hart-Rudman study, that said we would get hit by terrorism in the next five years.

"This debate was going on in the mainstream of the Department of Defense as we were struggling for survival. What we picked up from that debate was this: 'We need to define those asymmetric threats as they pertain to our mission.' "

"We thought the primary threat was some sort of poor-man's cruise missile or Unmanned Aerial Vehicle from a commercial ship off the coast, maybe some old rickety freighter out in the Gulf," Scott says. "And in one of our briefings, we pointed out that for $83,000 you can buy an Unmanned Aerial Vehicle with GPS (Global Positioning System) navigation.

"These guys aren't looking for pinpoint accuracy. If you launch it into a metropolitan area, it's good enough. The objective is to kill Americans, as many as you can. That's what we were targeting."

The 1st Air Force mission brief — the basic presentation explaining what air sovereignty is

Photo by Lans Stout for Code One magazine

The mission of the 144th Fighter Wing, California Air National Guard, and nine other fighter units assigned to 1st Air Force and the Continental United States NORAD Region, would be turned upside down Sept. 11, 2001.

about — spoke to this scary reality. "As we started talking about Osama bin Laden, the examples we gave in our mission brief were the first World Trade Center bombing, the Tokyo Subway, Oklahoma City bombing, and Atlanta Olympics," Scott says. "What we did was connect those dots. The conclusion we drew was that we had a viable threat."

The military buzzword, actually an acronym, defined the latest risk: CBRNE — Chemical, Biological, Radiological, Nuclear, and Enhanced High Explosive — weapons, Navin says. "Ages ago, we knew who the enemy was," he says. "Later, there was recognition on our part that terrorism was a threat, but we thought it was a cruise missile threat."

How and where would the threat happen? Arnold

tried to get in the minds of the terrorists. His "El Paso example" spoke to the nation's vulnerability. The geographical hole between alert sites in Houston and Riverside, Calif., was so large that he wouldn't be able to protect El Paso, Texas, with fighter jets if the need immediately arose.

Adds Scott: "There was no military air threat from Mexico, but ... an asymmetric threat from Mexico. Our experience within Mexico with our counterdrug operation is that there are hundreds of unmanned little airfields you can get into and out of very easily.

"Major General Arnold believed that if a terrorist called and said in one hour he would overfly El Paso and spray deadly gas, we would watch it live on CNN because we could not get aircraft to that location in time to stop it."

□□□

At times it seems like Arnold and his staff were gazing into a crystal ball. But, Arnold points out, "we thought the terrorist attack would come from outside the United States."

Training exercises at 1st Air Force continued to that effect, and occasionally a serious incident would arise. With all eyes focused outside, a tragedy inside foreshadowed the massive coordination required to handle air operations over our own soil.

On Oct. 25, 1999, professional golfer Payne Stewart was killed in a plane crash two miles west of Mina, S.D. The Lear 35 jet, flying from Orlando, Fla., to Dallas, strayed off course over northern Florida and was heading northwest when it ran out of fuel. The plane, believed to have lost cabin pressure, was tracked by the Southeast Air Defense Sector and later the Western Air Defense Sector. Fighter pilots from the 119th Fighter Wing, North Dakota Air National Guard, were scrambled by the Northeast Air Defense Sector. But it wasn't just 1st Air Force involved that day: Regular Air Force pilots from Eglin Air Force Base, Fla., and Guardsmen from Tulsa, Okla., helped escort the doomed airplane and assist the FAA, which had requested the military's help.

The day ended badly, Arnold says, but "the significant thing was we could not see that aircraft and the sectors worked with the FAA to track the airplane and feed information to us. Using the FAA radar and FAA positioning in order to use our fighters, we were able to divert them from training missions and get units like Fargo (119th Fighter Wing) to escort

> *"We thought the primary threat was some sort of poor-man's cruise missile or Unmanned Aerial Vehicle from a commercial ship off the coast, maybe some old rickety freighter out in the Gulf."*
>
> **— Retired Col. William A. Scott, former 1st Air Force vice commander**

the plane. What this proved to us is that we couldn't see and couldn't talk to each other over the central part of the United States."

Had the incident happened over a weekend, chances are military fighters wouldn't have been able to assist, Scott says. "This happened on a normal workday," he adds. "And the event led the public to believe we were much more ready than we were. This was a mini-scenario where we were garnering nontraditional 1st Air Force forces to execute an operational mission."

Not two years later, an operational mission on a much larger scale would unfold over the continental United States. That day — Sept. 11, 2001 — would end horribly.

Terror's eve

The day before America was attacked, NORAD was ready for war. The command was participating in an annual exercise called "Vigilant Guardian." It was practice. It was war games that would end with lessons on how to fight the better fight. This make-believe air war would happen off America's shores. This was not an air war over America.

"As much as you brief what could happen in the future, I think from an intellectual standpoint, we realized the greatest threat to the United States prior to Sept. 11, 2001, was going to be a terrorist attack," Arnold reflects one year after the tragedy. "But I did not envision that it would be hijacked airplanes run into buildings like that. I thought maybe a plane would be stolen and come from outside the United States and have a biological or chemical or nuclear weapon aboard. That was our thought. That is what our mission was about. Our mission was not about the internal threat. It was about the external threat."

Hijackings were regarded as a law enforcement — not military — issue, and "in the NORAD business, we were looking outward at things coming into this country, and that is what we practiced in exercises," Arnold says. "We practiced how to get that airplane to land or how to get approval to shoot it down. ... No, we did not envision people hijacking airplanes from within the United States, taking over those aircraft and using them as fuel-air bombs."

But when the unforeseeable happened Sept. 11, America's military was able to respond because the air sovereignty mission had been preserved, adds former Air National Guard director Shepperd. "The transition of 1st Air Force to Air National Guard control gave us the ability to maintain air sovereignty in our country," Shepperd says. "Thank goodness we had the Air National Guard on Sept. 11. Had we taken down our entire air defense structure, we would never have been able to do what we did and wouldn't have had command and control or liaison with the FAA."

On that tragic day, America's air defense forces in the air and on the ground worked closely with the FAA to clear the skies of terror. "In less than an hour ... the whole world changed," says Col. Bob Marr, commander of the Northeast Air Defense Sector, who would watch young airmen at the radar scopes as they scrambled the fighters, hoping against hope they'd make it to the World Trade Center and Pentagon on time.

The air war over America had begun. The exercise was over.

Staff Sgt. Keith Driessen, crew chief, 119th Fighter Wing, North Dakota Air National Guard, performs a preflight inspection on an F-16 "Fighting Falcon."

1 Paul E. McAllister, *TAC Strategic Air Defense Reference Book: October 1979-December 1989* (Langley Air Force Base, Va.: Headquarters 1st Air Force, 1990), 7-8.

2 William A. Scott, conversation with author, 31 July 2002.

3 McAllister, *TAC Strategic Air Defense Reference Book*, 14.

4 United States Air Force, *Air Force Basic Doctrine* (Headquarters Air Force Doctrine Center, Maxwell Air Force Base, Ala., 1997), 69.

5 Thomas Fuller, "NORAD at 40: Historical Overview" (North American Aerospace Defense Command History Office, 1997), n.p.

6 Ibid., n.p.

7 Paul Connors, "The Third Activation: First Air Force from 1985 to 1991" (monograph, 1st Air Force History Office, 1999), n.p.

8 Air Force Space Command, History of United States Space Command, Aerospace Defense Command: January-December 1985 (Air Force Space Command History Office), 212-213.

9 Connors, "The Third Activation: First Air Force from 1985 to 1991," n.p.

10 Ibid., n.p.

11 Ibid., n.p.

12 Lawrence R. Benson, "Golden Legacy, Boundless Future: A Brief History of the United States Air Force" (Air Force History Support Office), n.p., n.d.

13 Leslie Filson, *Sovereign Skies: Air National Guard Takes Command of 1st Air Force* (1st Air Force Public Affairs Office, 1999), 4.

14 Ibid., 113.

15 Ibid., 5-6.

16 Ibid., 11.

17 Ibid., 17.

18 Don Arias, Dan Navin and William A. Scott, conversation with author, 16 April 2002.

19 Filson, *Sovereign Skies*, 23.

20 Ibid., 85.

21 Ibid., 97.

22 William S. Cohen, "Report of the Quadrennial Defense Review" (Washington, D.C., Department of Defense, May 1997), Section 5.

23 Scott, conversation with author.

24 Ibid.

25 Dan Navin and William A. Scott, interview with author, conference call, Tyndall Air Force Base, Fla., 15 July 2002.

26 Gary Hart and Warren B. Rudman, "New World Coming: American Security in the 21st Century" (the United States Commission on National Security/21st Century, September 1999), Phase 1.

27 Ibid., Phase 1.

Photo by Master Sgt. William Quinn, 119th Fighter Wing, North Dakota Air National Guard

CHAPTER 3

9.11.01

Air war over America begins

Photo by Lt. Col. Bill Ramsay, 102nd Fighter Wing, Massachusetts Air National Guard

U.S. Navy photo by Journalist 1st Class Preston Keres

46   AIR WAR OVER AMERICA

DAY OF TERROR:
Nation's air controllers, military fliers and crews fight for America's skies

*I*t *should have been a perfect day. The skies were clear, blue and beautiful with miles and miles of visibility across the northeast. But what should have been was not. The day's beauty would become ugly and all clarity would fade to a murky fog of hatred, turmoil and terror.*

□□□

Desperate plea

Massachusetts Air National Guard pilot Lt. Col. Tim Duffy remembers driving into work the morning of Sept. 11, 2001, disappointed he wasn't on the flying schedule. As he drove through the gate at Otis Air National Guard Base on Cape Cod, he admired the "clear-in-a-million" skies any pilot would crave. It was a pretty — even gorgeous — Tuesday, a great day to fly. Duffy never could have dreamed up the scenario that would unfold in only a few hours, never could have imagined what he'd see from his F-15 cockpit 5,000 feet above Manhattan that crisp fall morning.

Around 8:30 a.m., a Federal Aviation Administration controller in Boston phoned the control tower at Otis with a serious request: American Airlines Flight 11 had lost its identification signal and appeared headed toward Manhattan. It looked like a possible hijacking, and fighters were needed — fast.

The Associated Press

Above: A fiery image is caught on film at the World Trade Center Sept. 11, 2001.

Left: Firefighters walk past the American flag as they work their way toward the heart of the devastation that was once the World Trade Center, Sept. 14, 2001.

Previous page: A pair of F-15s assigned to the 102nd Fighter Wing, Massachusetts Air National Guard; F-16s from the 158th Fighter Wing, Vermont Air National Guard; and a KC-135 from the 101st Air Refueling Wing, Maine Air National Guard; fly a Combat Air Patrol mission over New York City.

The Pentagon in flames just minutes after a hijacked jetliner crashed into the building Sept. 11, 2001.

U.S. Marine Corps photo by Cpl. Jason Ingersoll

The 102nd Fighter Wing at Otis was one of seven alert sites in the continental United States, with two loaded airplanes ready for immediate take-off.

"It didn't happen the way it was supposed to or the way you would hope it would come down," Duffy says. "But the way it came down ... it really didn't hurt us at all. We were the ones who were contacted right away and knew about it before the air defense sector."

"About 8:30, 8:35 out by the ops (operations) desk, I got a phone call from one of the sergeants," he continues. "He said, 'Duffy, you have a phone call from tower. ... Something about a hijacking.' As soon as we heard there was something about a hijacking we got moving. That's not something we throw around lightly, that word. I had the radio with me; we call it the brick. ... So I called for 'Nasty' (Maj. Dan Nash) and I to suit up right away."

Lt. Col. Jon Treacy, commander of the wing's 101st Fighter Squadron, phoned NEADS — the Northeast Air Defense Sector — in Rome, N.Y., to report the FAA's request. The sector commander would have authority to scramble the airplanes. But the FAA had already gotten through to a young tech sergeant at NEADS just reporting for duty that morning. Jeremy Powell answered a call he will never forget.

NEADS: *"Huntress Weapons, Sgt. Powell."*

FAA: *"All right, Boston Center, we have a problem here. We have a hijacked aircraft headed towards New York and we need you guys to, we need someone to scramble F-16s or something to help us out."*

NEADS: *"Is this real-world or an exercise?"*

FAA: *"No, this is real-world, this is not an exercise, not a test."* [1]

"I think about that phone call constantly," Powell, since promoted to lieutenant, says. "I think about it all the time."

□□□

If normal procedures had taken place that morning, Powell probably wouldn't have taken that phone call. Normally, the FAA would have contacted officials at the Pentagon's National Military Command Center who would have contacted the North American Aerospace Defense Command. The secretary of defense would have had to approve the use of military assets to assist in a hijacking, always considered a law enforcement issue. [2] But nothing was normal on Sept. 11, 2001, and many say the traditional chain of command went by the wayside to get the job done.

Around the country that morning and many mornings before, 14 fighter jets were loaded and ready to intercept unidentified aircraft approaching the United States. Military controllers at three air defense sectors — in the northeast, southeast and

Above: Medical personnel and volunteers work the first medical triage area set up outside the Pentagon after American Airlines Flight 77 crashed into the southwest corner of the building Sept. 11, 2001.

Left: 2nd Lt. Jeremy Powell of the Northeast Air Defense Sector in Rome, N.Y., — a technical sergeant at the time — took an unforgettable phone call from the Federal Aviation Administration Sept. 11, 2001. The FAA was requesting assistance in intercepting the hijackers.

west — were monitoring the air picture, only a hot line call away from pilots on immediate alert. First Air Force and the Continental United States NORAD Region had protected America's air borders for years. But the command hadn't trained for fighting enemies within, hadn't practiced for coordinated attacks in continental airspace — the radars were always looking outward.

When terrorists took over the skies on Sept. 11, 2001, America's military reacted swiftly. In the northeast, massive efforts began to get every fighter available into the air. Controllers at the Western Air Defense Sector in Washington and Southeast Air Defense Sector in Florida sent fighter pilots into their cockpits to await further orders. Military air controllers worked hand-in-hand with the FAA trying to find possibly hijacked airliners. Military tankers and Airborne Warning and Control System aircraft provided crucial refueling and radar support throughout the day and beyond.

The military response was tremendous on Sept. 11, 2001, and everyone has a story to share of remarkable achievement amid terror and tragedy. But this story focuses mostly on the Air National Guard members who protected America's air borders before that defining autumn day.

That community grew to astonishing strengths in a matter of hours as the 14 aircraft on alert increased to more than 400 fighters, tankers and airborne early warning platforms. [3] Naval warships reinforced that presence as they kept watch in the Pacific, Atlantic and Gulf of Mexico.

Armed with a sense of patriotism, pride and volunteerism, the military response was tremendous on Sept. 11, 2001, but with thousands of lives lost and ruined in a calculated terrorist attack, it was a bittersweet triumph.

Above: An F-15 "Eagle" assigned to the 102nd Fighter Wing, Massachusetts Air National Guard, departs the runway at Otis Air National Guard Base. The wing was the first to scramble and fly Combat Air Patrols over New York Sept. 11, 2001.

Right: A crew chief from the 102nd Fighter Wing maintenance squadron gives a pilot the signal to crank the engine before taxiing down the runway for takeoff.

Photos by Staff Sgt. Sandra Niedzwiecki, 102nd Fighter Wing, Massachusetts Air National Guard

Lt. Col. Ian Sanderson, Northeast Air Defense Sector chief of operations control, says the Sept. 11 hijackings were unlike anything personnel there had trained for. The hijackings didn't fit the usual profile, he says.

Senior Master Sgt. Robert Von Hagen attaches wings to an AIM-120/AMRAAM — Advanced Medium Range Air-to-Air Missile — loaded on a wingtip launcher Sept. 11, 2001, at the 119th Fighter Wing, North Dakota Air National Guard. Master Sgt. Bradley Johnson, 119th Logistics Group quality assurance inspector, observes. At far left is 119th Fighter Wing Vice Commander Col. Thomas E. Larson. The "Happy Hooligans" provided F-16 combat capability following the terrorist attacks.

Mad scramble

In a strange twist of fate, that very morning the command and control technicians at NEADS were beginning a 12-hour shift for the NORAD exercise "Vigilant Guardian." Across the command from Alaska to Canada and throughout the continental United States, battle staffs were poised to fight the simulated air war. The unusually high state of readiness was a sheer stroke of luck, many would say later, as commanders made unprecedented decisions with astonishing speed and airmen did everything they could to identify and intercept the hijackers.

"Around 8:40 there was a huddle of people around one of the scopes," says Col. Bob Marr, NEADS commander. "I've seen many exercises ... and as I saw that huddle I said, 'There's got to be something wrong, something is happening here.' You usually see that whenever they find a track on the scope that looks unusual; it's usually an indicator that something is getting ready to kick off."

From the battle cab — a glass-walled room overlooking the dimly lighted sector floor — Marr thought the hubbub was part of the exercise. He sent Lt. Col. Dawne Deskins, mission crew commander, to check it out. She came running back, Marr says, with urgency in her voice: the FAA needed help with a possible hijacking; a civilian airliner had just disappeared from the scope and was headed toward New York.

"At this point our mind-set was the 1970s-vintage hijack," Deskins says. "We didn't have a huge concern this aircraft was going to crash. We were thinking, 'let's get some airplanes up to support it, escort it and figure out where it's going to land.'"

Marr ordered Otis F-15 pilots Duffy and Nash to battle stations — pilots in the cockpits with engines turned off. He says the fliers were halfway to their jets when he phoned his boss, Maj. Gen. Larry K. Arnold, 1st Air Force and CONR commander.

Arnold remembers the phone call well. "By the

Photo by Scott A. Gwilt, Daily Sentinel, Rome, N.Y.

A tracker "on scope" in the darkened operations room at the Northeast Air Defense Sector, Rome, N.Y. Airmen at NEADS were doing all they could to track and intercept the hijackers on Sept. 11.

time I talked to Bob Marr, he said he had the jets on battle stations and would like to get them airborne," he recalls. "I said, 'Go ahead and scramble them and we'll get authorities later.' ... He scrambled them and in the meantime I picked up the phone and talked to the operations deputy up at NORAD and he said, 'Yeah, we'll work this with the National Military Command Center. Go ahead and scramble the aircraft.' "

It was unfamiliar territory, but Marr knew what he had to do. "My intent was to scramble Otis to military airspace while we found out what was going on," he says.

□□□

Somewhere on the radar scopes was American Airlines Flight 11, which had deviated from its Boston-Los Angeles flight plan and was not communicating with FAA ground controllers. Workers at the FAA Boston Center were baffled: The pilots weren't talking and a strange, possibly foreign, voice could be heard saying, *"We have some planes."* [4] It was fast becoming a frightening situation. The crew at NEADS was desperate to track and intercept the plane.

"When we received that call, all eyes were over New York looking for search tracks," says NEADS Staff Sgt. Larry Thornton, whose job until then had been searching for incoming flights over the ocean. Those "search tracks" can be tough to locate jumbled among hundreds of cooperative aircraft emitting electronic signatures to the radar scopes.

"Once we were called by the FAA, we could find split-second hits on what we thought we were looking for," Thornton says. "But the area was so congested and it was incredibly difficult to find. We were looking for little dash marks in a pile of clutter and a pile of aircraft on a two-dimensional scope."

Each fluorescent green pulsating dot on the scope represented an airplane, and there were thousands out there, especially over the busy north-

The Pentagon burns into the night of Sept. 11.

east United States. To complicate matters, the sector didn't share much of the FAA's interior radar data, especially at low altitudes, and had to piece together the incoming information. But Master Sgt. Joe McCain believes they saw Flight 11 disappear over New York that morning. "We picked up a search track going down the Hudson Valley, straight in from the north toward New York," he says. "It's very unusual to find a search target, which is a plane with its transponder turned off, in that area. This plane was headed toward New York going faster than the average Cessna and was no doubt a jet aircraft. We had many clues. The plane was fast and heading in an unusual direction with no bea-

U.S. Navy photo by Photographer's Mate 2nd Class Robert Houlihan

nocent victims were killed that day.

It was the moment the sleeping dragon of the world's most powerful military was awakened with a start — much as it was 60 years earlier on Dec. 7, 1941. As the scramble lights flashed green at Otis Air National Guard Base, a new kind of war was beginning. When the F-15s took off with fire igniting behind them, flight lead Duffy told his wingman they would fly supersonic. It wasn't standard procedure, but the Gulf War veteran was filled with an irresistible sense of urgency. "This is one of those things I can't really explain why I did it the way I did it," Duffy says. "When we took off I left it in full afterburner the whole time. So we climbed up, we were supersonic going down to Long Island and 'Nasty' (Nash) called and said, 'Hey Duff, you're super,' and I said, 'Yeah, I know, don't worry about it.'

"At the time I just wanted to get there ... we were high enough that we wouldn't blow out windows or do any damage to anything. I figured if anyone cared later I could probably take the heat for trying to get there quickly. Again, we have no idea what we are going toward. We are taking off to go help somebody and we needed to get there quickly to assess the situation."

They didn't know American Airlines Flight 11 had just plunged into the twin towers.

Under attack

Could this be the airplane the NEADS controllers were so desperately tracking?

Deskins says they just couldn't be sure. "Our first question was, 'Are we talking about this hijacked aircraft?' " she says. "Our identification section was asking what type of aircraft it was and Boston Center was reporting American 11 still airborne. So we thought it must have been a weird coincidence."

But her gut told her differently: "I remember thinking, 'Oh boy, this is starting to sound really

con. We had raw radar data only. Everything just kind of fit. We watched that track until it faded over New York City and right after that someone came out of the break room and said the World Trade Center had been hit."

On Cape Cod, 160 miles to the northeast, the F-15 pilots were ordered to scramble. As the jets rolled down Runway 5 at Otis Air National Guard Base, American Airlines Flight 11, a Boeing 767 with 92 people aboard, perished in the clear blue Manhattan sky. It was 8:46 a.m. Eastern Standard Time, a tragic tick of the clock that forever seared itself into the American psyche. It was the unforgettable moment when the first of hundreds of in-

Photo by Tech. Sgt. Mark Olsen, New Jersey Department of Military and Veterans Affairs Public Affairs Office

The 1st Battalion, 150th Aviation, New Jersey Army National Guard, begins post-attack flight operations over New York in a UH-60A "Blackhawk" helicopter Sept. 11, 2001.

bad,'" Deskins continues. "I didn't want to jump to any conclusions but it seemed logical that the hijacked aircraft had hit the World Trade Center."

Without much to go on, the NEADS controllers continued to search in vain, struggling to lead the Massachusetts pilots toward the airliner. "I was fighting to get the (plane's) tail number," says Master Sgt. Maureen Dooley, noncommissioned officer in charge of identification technicians. "We were trying to grab at anything we could."

And when the FAA reported that Flight 11 had indeed crashed, Dooley says she felt helpless. "I think everybody did. We were doing everything in our power." 5

Marr remembers thinking that it must have been a horrible accident. Maybe the pilot had flown too low and lost control upon descent into John F. Kennedy International Airport, N.Y., he reasoned. "I'm thinking this is probably an accident because

there's been a hijack," Marr says. "The guy is going to JFK and every hijack to this date has been an individual who wants to land an airplane somewhere other than where it's supposed to land. ... So we surmise there's been a terrible accident and there's not much we can do about it."

But uncertainty and doubt remained. Says NEADS chief of operations control Lt. Col. Ian Sanderson: "When we got word of the first crash, I heard it but I didn't believe it. I had to go down the hall and look at the TV. And what I remember most is that the hijacking didn't follow the expected profile. It wasn't the type of hijacking we'd trained for. I was thinking, 'this doesn't taste right, feel right or smell right.'"

With the Massachusetts F-15s still headed toward Manhattan, Marr notified New York Air National Guard headquarters to report what he knew. "Our jets are heading down south toward

Whiskey 105 and we don't really have a mission for them at this point, because we don't have any other problems in the air," Marr says.

Whiskey 105, the military training airspace southeast of Long Island, "would put them within a few minutes of New York City to 'CAP' (Combat Air Patrol), burn down gas and wait for further instructions," Marr says. "By this time we start getting CNN showing in the battle cab ... and as we're watching the television we see another aircraft come into view and hit the second tower of the World Trade Center."

□□□

Disbelief filled the room. Everyone was floored, Sanderson says: "We had to sort of wrest back control." [6]

Adds Deskins: "That plane came out of nowhere ... we didn't even know there was a second hijack. Now we knew it was intentional."

From the CONR Air Operations Center at Tyndall Air Force Base, Fla., Arnold and his staff were stunned as they watched the same live images. "When I saw the second plane hit, my thought at the time was, 'My God, was that a replay of the first one?' " Arnold says. "Then I realized there were two smoking holes and not one, and at that time, I think all of us thought it was beyond the realm of probability for two accidents to occur like that. We were under attack at this time."

United Airlines Flight 175 crashed into the south tower of the World Trade Center at 9:03 a.m. with 65 people aboard. Two 767s were gone and it was anyone's guess what might happen next.

"I thought it might be prudent to pull out of the exercise, which we did," Arnold says. "We called NORAD and they were well aware of what had happened obviously. ... As we pulled out of the exercise we were getting calls about United Flight 93 and we were worried about that. Then we had another call from Boston Center about a possible hijacking, but that turned out to be the airplane that had already hit the south tower but we didn't know

that at the time."

At the NORAD command center near Colorado Springs, Colo., an air threat conference call was beginning. Open communication lines were established between top U.S. and Canadian officials to eventually include President George W. Bush, Vice President Dick Cheney and Secretary of Defense Donald Rumsfeld. [7] Arnold would find himself on that call when the last suspicious airplane had landed. But that wouldn't be for hours.

In the darkened operations center at NEADS, Marr and the operations crew felt the gravity of

Photo by Scott A. Gwilt, Daily Sentinel, Rome, N.Y.

Lt. Col. Dawne Deskins, Northeast Air Defense Sector mission crew commander, was tracking the movement of American Airlines Flight 77 on Sept. 11, 2001. She had six or seven radar hits before watching the plane's signal fade and disappear from the scope.

the situation. "We had both buildings hit and didn't have any other aircraft at this time except Otis, heading to the World Trade Center in a straight line," Marr says. "At Mach 1 it would take them 16 minutes to get there, that's 10 miles a minute."

Approaching Manhattan, Duffy and Nash were still pursuing Flight 11, trying to get information from NEADS on the plane's location. "I call for bogey dope (target information) and I don't realize American has already hit," Duffy says. "So I'm still chasing American and ... we're going right down Long Island and three or four minutes later I call for bogey dope again and right then they say the second aircraft just hit the World Trade Center. So, confusion in my cockpit: *The second aircraft?*

"I look up and we're about 60 or 70 miles outside Manhattan and I can see the towers burning. ... OK, obviously everything just changed from my personal mind-set. We take off to go help somebody, and now as I look up and can see the burning I say, 'OK, now people are dying.'

"It's kind of hard to explain, but basically you switch into a combat mode where you say, 'OK, this just got real serious real fast.' ... Now people are dying and you're thinking, 'OK, what do I have to do?' And you have to put emotion aside because you don't have time for it."

Hard to believe only a few hours earlier Duffy was thinking about the weather on his drive in to work. "It was one of the prettiest days I've ever flown, literally there was not a cloud in the sky and visibility was probably better than a hundred miles," Duffy says. "It was just crystal clear. When I was driving in that morning and knew I wasn't on the flying schedule I was thinking, 'Oh what a day, what a day to go flying.' "

Now the pilots were shocked and amazed as they watched the smoldering scene below. "We

> "As the F-15s go over the city, now the fog of war is starting to set in."
>
> — Col. Bob Marr, commander,
> Northeast Air Defense Sector

were going as fast as the airplanes could go," Nash says, then hesitates. "We did everything we could but unfortunately couldn't stop anything."

The F-15s were loaded with extra weapons and fuel because of the exercise and "were ready to engage anything if they had to," Marr says. "But obviously this is peacetime and we have no authority to engage any targets ... but we're thinking New York City is under attack."

More jets would be needed. The NORAD "deep peace" stance meant only two East Coast fighters remained on alert. They were from a detachment of the 119th Fighter Wing, North Dakota Air National Guard. The alert facility at Langley Air Force Base, Va., is several hundred miles from Manhattan, but Marr directed the pilots to battle stations anyway. "The plan was to protect New York City," Marr says.

As tensions continued to build, the FAA took unprecedented measures to clear the skies of the northeast United States. "Air Traffic Control Zero" would soon follow across the nation. [8]

"Now our (Massachusetts) pilots are chasing down traffic that is trying to get on the ground or to Boston or New York," Marr says. "We didn't know what could have been cruise-missile airliners.

"As the F-15s go over the city, now the fog of war is starting to set in."

On the cool sector floor at NEADS, that fog was thick with misinformation, fear and apprehen-

What is left of the south tower of the World Trade Center in New York City stands like a tombstone among the debris and devastation caused by the Sept. 11 terrorist attack.

U.S. Navy photo by Journalist 1st Class Preston Keres

U.S. Army photos by Staff Sgt. John Valceanu

Family members visit the Pentagon Sept. 15, 2001, to pay respects to their loved ones who died in the Sept. 11 attack there.

sion. Many of the phone calls coming in were rumors and there was little way to confirm or deny them. The pilots above Manhattan, meanwhile, were wondering what would come next as they watched the devastation below.

"As soon as I saw the towers burning, I called up Huntress (NEADS) and said 'Huntress, 4, 5, say mission,' " Duffy says. " 'What do you want me to do next? What do you need from me right this second?' ... He didn't know what to do."

Huntress would soon have more information: "It only took a couple minutes of us in the area before they came back on and said 'NORAD just took control of all the airspace in the country,' " Duffy says. " 'Proceed direct to Manhattan and set up Combat Air Patrol.' I said, 'OK, got that.' "

The pilots requested and were immediately given clearance from the FAA to fly at any altitude necessary. "They just gave us the airspace," Duffy says.

FAA: *"We shut all traffic off at Boston Center, no one departing, and we're rerouting all JFK arrivals and Newark Metro airport's (N.J.)."*

NEADS: *"Copy sir."*

FAA: *"I do have a question for you: In case we have any more aircraft that start deviating, we need to know, do you have anyone on alert or is that something that you can do just in case this happens to any more aircraft?"*

NEADS: *"... I've got fighters in Whiskey 105 right now, and I've got a tanker there as well, I've got other aircraft on alert at Langley as well, I'm getting ready to, I've got trackers over JFK, over Boston and that area, just looking for anything suspicious."*

FAA: *"Anything suspicious, OK, and we'll let you know about the internationals. We're not sure what we're doing about them yet."* 9

With little time to grasp what had happened in New York, the FAA continued to report more shocking information to the Northeast sector: American Airlines Flight 77 and Delta Airlines Flight 1989, both 767s bound for Los Angeles, were possibly hijacked. Somewhere over Cleveland, United Airlines Flight 93 bound for San Francisco was still off course.

"The FAA is starting to report more aircraft not following their flight plans," Marr says. "Now we are looking at a host of potential problems. Then we get another call from Boston Center that we have a problem near Washington and 'you'd better check on it.' "

The North Dakota alert pilots were still in their cockpits at Langley Air Force Base. At the squadron operations desk, young F-16 pilot Capt. Craig Borgstrom took a terse phone call from NEADS. "The guy from the sector asked me, 'How many can you get airborne right now?' " Borgstrom recalls. "I told him I had two on battle stations. He then said, 'That's not what I asked. How many total airplanes can you send up?'

"I said, 'I'll give you three.'

"And he said, 'Then go!' "

Just as Borgstrom grabbed his gear to join the others, the Klaxon alarm sounded and the red lights turned green in the alert barn. The active air scramble order had been given. It was 9:24 a.m. and the planes were given highest priority over all other air traffic at Langley Air Force Base. 10

"We crank and scramble ... we took off, the three of us, and basically the formation we always brief on alert, we'll stay in a two- to three-mile trail from the guy in front," Borgstrom says. "They (NEADS) were giving us the heading and altitude

Right: The Northeast Air Defense Sector called upon the Michigan Air National Guard 127th Wing on Sept. 11, 2001. Two pilots from the Selfridge unit were flying a training mission and would have been asked to intercept United Airlines Flight 93 had it not turned toward Pennsylvania. In this photo taken a few months later, 2nd Lt. Christopher Melka gives the "ready to roll" sign.

Below: An F-15 "Eagle" from the 125th Fighter Wing, Florida Air National Guard, refuels from a KC-135 "Stratotanker" on a Combat Air Patrol mission over central Florida on Dec. 5, 2001. The Jacksonville-based wing is one of 10 assigned to 1st Air Force and the Continental United States NORAD Region.

U.S. Air Force photo by Tech. Sgt. Shaun Withers

AIR WAR OVER AMERICA

of north-northeast up to 20,000 feet. Then shortly after takeoff they changed our heading more northwesterly and gave us max-subsonic.

"That's as fast as you can go without breaking the sound barrier. I've never heard it before in my short career, but I don't think anyone's heard that order before."

The F-16s were being vectored toward Washington, D.C., instead of New York. As they were scrambling, Deskins was watching a suspicious track on the radar scope. "I had the scope focused in on the D.C. area and got blips of this aircraft that appeared to be going in a turn around D.C.," she says. "It was going fast for where it was located and I remember looking at the guy next to me and saying, *'What is that?'*

"I probably got six or seven radar returns on it before it faded and was just gone. You're thinking, 'What just happened?' I got this feeling in the pit of my stomach and said, 'That's another one.'"

Tech. Sgt. Ronald G. Belluscio, a NEADS se-

nior weapons director technician, sent the F-16s to Washington that morning. "When all of this was happening, we were giving directions as enlisted personnel," he says. "We were empowered and entrusted to certain tasks that we aren't normally accustomed to doing to get the job done. I jumped on a frequency, per the senior director, and was told to ask the Langley birds to vector over the Pentagon. I didn't know it had been hit."

Majs. Dean Eckmann, Brad Derrig and Borgstrom continued flying max-subsonic. "The sector gave us certain coordinates to CAP over a certain point," Borgstrom says. "We all dialed in the coordinates to figure out exactly where we were going and we got to our point and we could see from ... maybe 40 miles out, smoke billowing. We started putting things together.

"OK, we're going toward where that smoke is and as you get closer, you start thinking, 'OK, maybe there's some type of attack going on.' You start correlating Washington, D.C., with New York.

We still have no 'intel' brief of what's going on ... and another building is on fire. ... We knew something terribly wrong was going on. Something severe had happened."

American Airlines Flight 77, with 64 people aboard, had crashed into the Pentagon at 9:38 a.m., but the pilots didn't know that. Borgstrom thought maybe a gas line had burst or a car bomb had exploded. But their mission, he says, was clear: keep all airplanes away from Washington, D.C.

The three pilots, all on different frequencies but sharing a common intra-flight channel, were hearing a lot of chatter but nothing about airliners crashing into buildings, Borgstrom says. "There was some confusion for us, this was very abnormal," he continues. "We were all three on different frequencies ... and were getting orders from a lot of different people."

Only a few minutes after reaching the Washington area, flight lead Eckmann was vectored toward two low-flying aircraft. It was around 9:45 a.m. [11] "As we're coming in, I set up a Combat Air Patrol with air traffic controllers and they come back to me and say there are a couple unknowns heading north on the Potomac River toward the White House," Eckmann says. "We were up in the high 20s and I basically roll inverted and go straight down. It took no time to get there and I get a radar contact on one of them and end up identifying them. One is a military helicopter and the other is a law enforcement helicopter and they're obviously heading toward the Pentagon to aid."

Eckmann flew low over the Capitol and Mall area. "I wanted to clear the area and make sure nothing else was coming in," he says. "I was also looking on the ground for something suspicious and thought if I saw a big fuel tanker truck heading toward the White House I could possibly take him

Arkansas Air National Guard photo by Tech. Sgt. Randy L. Byrd

out with my gun. You have so many thoughts racing through your mind. ... While I'm doing this, Craig (Borgstrom) calls me and says Huntress wants to know the extent of the damage at the Pentagon.

"I fly by the Washington Monument and turn back down and fly over the Pentagon, just to the south of the Pentagon, and tell them the two outer rings have been damaged," Eckmann says. "They asked me if I knew what it was and I told them I guessed it was a big fuel tanker truck because of the amount of smoke and flames coming up and nobody indicated anything about an airplane. And there was no airplane wreckage off to the side."

Eckmann says the scene below was shockingly surreal. "It was almost a feeling of disbelief," he says. "Kind of like watching a bad movie. You can't believe what you're seeing, but you're still watching it."

Eckmann would later hear that the presence of a fully loaded F-16 darting overhead was a great comfort to people below. "A lot of people said it made them feel safe," he says. "They looked up and saw an armed F-16 and I guess they started cheering. I heard stories that people went back in after seeing me fly over to help others out. What would have happened had I stayed up high? They wouldn't have seen me. Now they knew they were safe. It was pure luck that I happened to be down

Right: An F-15 assigned to the Massachusetts Air National Guard 102nd Fighter Wing flies a Combat Air Patrol mission over New York City.

Above: An AMRAAM missile is loaded on an F-16 assigned to the 188th Fighter Wing, Arkansas Air National Guard.

Photo by Lt. Col. Bill Ramsay, 102nd Fighter Wing, Massachusetts Air National Guard

there and called on that initial intercept."

Shortly, Eckmann would hear an extraordinary request: *"Protect the House."* A Secret Service agent arrived at one of Washington's Air Traffic Control towers and wanted to talk to the flight lead.

"I took it to mean protect the White House," Eckmann says.

Clearance to kill

With all available alert fighters in the air, Marr and his crew were still faced with United Flight 93. The plane was headed west, so controllers began looking for any other fighter jets that might be nearby. "We don't have fighters that way and we think he's headed toward Detroit or Chicago," Marr says. "I'm thinking Chicago is the target and know that Selfridge Air National Guard Base (Mich.) has F-16s in the air. We contacted them so they could head off 93 at the pass. The idea is to get in there, close in on him and convince him to turn. ... As United Airlines Flight 93 was going out, we received the clearance to kill if need be. In fact, Major General Arnold's words almost verbatim were: *'We will take lives in the air to save lives on the ground.'*"

But the Selfridge pilots — not part of the NORAD air sovereignty force — were unarmed. Lt. Col. Tom Froling and Maj. Douglas Champagne of the 127th Wing had just fired the last of their 20mm cannon ammunition in routine training. They were oblivious to the events in New York and Washington but heard unusual conversation over their radio frequencies.

"Something strange was occurring and I couldn't put my finger on what was happening," Froling says.

A Vermont Air National Guard F-16 from the 158th Fighter Wing patrols the skies above New York City on Sept. 12, 2001.

U.S. Air Force photo by Lt. Col. Terry Moultrup

> *"Flying over Central Park at 1,000 feet and 500 knots ... trying to identify people, that's just wrong. You should never be doing this over downtown Manhattan, watching the towers burning."*
>
> **— Lt. Col. Tim Duffy, F-15 pilot, Massachusetts Air National Guard**

"I could hear (the FAA) Cleveland Center talking to the airlines and I started putting things together and knew something was up. Then our commander wanted to know if we'd expended our training ordnance. The only thing that went through my mind was maybe there was a problem with our airplane, maybe we missed something and shouldn't have been shooting the gun."

Froling didn't know he was being considered to shoot down an airliner. Without weapons and because United Flight 93 turned away from Chicago, he never faced that decision. The Michigan pilots would safely return to their base. Champagne remembers a squadron buddy running toward his jet as he was taxiing in. "I'll never forget this, it is one of the things I'll remember, I think forever," he says. "I was in the cockpit and I remember him mouthing the words to me, 'It's bad. It's really, really bad.'"

Above Manhattan, Duffy and Nash were given clearance to kill over their radio frequencies, but to this day aren't sure who gave that order. Was it NEADS or a civilian air traffic controller? [12] Uncertain, they continued to fly over the city.

"Flying over Central Park at 1,000 feet and 500 knots ... trying to identify people, that's just wrong. You should never be doing this over downtown Manhattan, watching the towers burning," Duffy says. "We're down over Newark getting people

U.S. Navy photo by Photographer's Mate 2nd Class Jim Watson

Above: A weary New York City firefighter surveys the destruction as he departs the area on Sept. 13, 2001. Emergency personnel worked tirelessly for more than 24 hours immediately following the Sept. 11 terrorist attacks that brought down the World Trade Center.

Right: Days after the attacks, a volunteer steel worker cuts a large part of debris to make it easier to haul away from the former site of the World Trade Center.

away from the airport, and of course we're trying to get them down on the ground, or identify them. As you're coming back, the Statue of Liberty with the towers burning behind it as we're flying around, you're saying to yourself, 'This is nuts.' "

Clearing the skies

"America was under attack," Marr says, and controllers were still grappling with two planes missing and frightening rumors of bomb threats and airplane crashes that really never happened. "In less than an hour here the whole world changed."

Amid the fog and madness, Arnold and his staff were on the phone with Marr; Col. John Cromwell, Western Air Defense Sector commander; and Col. Larry Kemp, Southeast Air Defense Sector commander. They were making fast decisions as the FAA reported more information. At one point during the four-hour ordeal, 21 planes were unaccounted for, Arnold says. "We were concerned about Flight 93 and this Delta aircraft (Flight 1989) and were trying to find aircraft in the vicinity to help out," Arnold recalls.

"We didn't know where it was going to go. We were concerned about Detroit ... and the fighters up there were out of gas with no armament. Then we called a Guard unit in Toledo, Ohio, because we thought 93 or Delta Flight 1989 might be headed toward Chicago. Then NEADS called another Guard unit in Syracuse, New York, and eventually got them moving in the direction of getting airplanes airborne.

"Then we watched the 93 track as it meandered around the Ohio-Pennsylvania area and started to turn south toward D.C. By now the Pentagon has been hit and we have aircraft on orbit, the 'Happy Hooligans' of the 119th at Fargo, North Dakota, (from the Langley alert detachment). They are now orbiting over Washington, D.C., and have been for awhile. As United 93 headed toward D.C., the desire is to move the fighters toward those aircraft.

Photo by Staff Sgt. Sandra Niedzwiecki, 102nd Fighter Wing, Massachusetts Air National Guard

Massachusetts Air National Guardsman Senior Airman Joel Milliken, 102nd Maintenance Weapons section, repairs an F-15 during Operation Noble Eagle.

But as we discussed it in the conference call, we decided not to move fighters toward 93 until it was closer because there could have been other aircraft coming in. By now a number of aircraft are being called possibly hijacked ... there was a lot of confusion, as you can imagine."

Missing planes seemed to be everywhere. "There were a number of false reports out there," Marr says. "What was valid? What was a guess? We just didn't know. ... We were in foreign territory; we are used to protecting the shores, way out overseas. Our processes and procedures weren't designed for this."

An obscure military plan, "SCATANA" — Security Control of Air Traffic and Air Navigation Aids — would help the FAA in its efforts to clear the skies. The commander of NORAD, Gen. Ralph E. Eberhart, ordered a limited version of the Cold War-era strategy, and allowed essential aircraft like rescue helicopters to fly. The decision was made during the air threat conference call and was backed by Transportation Secretary Norman Mineta. [13] The SCATANA order had been implemented only once before, and only for war games in 1961.

Through the fray, Marr remembers hearing that the FAA was evacuating its Cleveland Center. He didn't know why at the time and focused on United Flight 93, headed straight toward Washington. The North Dakota F-16s were loaded with missiles and hot guns and Marr was thinking about what these pilots might be expected to do. "United Airlines Flight 93 would not have hit Washington, D.C.," Marr says emphatically. "He would have been engaged and shot down before he got there."

Arnold concurs: "I had every intention of shooting down United 93 if it continued to progress toward Washington, D.C., and any other aircraft coming toward it that day, whether we had authority or not."

But as the story goes, the pilots were spared the unthinkable. With the now legendary "Let's Roll" rallying cry, the heroic passengers aboard United

Department of Defense photo

Ray Gould, Military District of Washington Engineers, stands in front of the exit point of American Airlines Flight 77 where it stopped moving through the Pentagon. The hijacked airliner had 64 people aboard and crashed at 9:38 a.m.

Airlines Flight 93 rushed the terrorists in the cockpit, bringing the airliner to the ground near Shanksville, Pa., at approximately 10:03 a.m. The Boeing 757, with 44 people aboard, reportedly dropped 1,200 feet in 12 seconds. [14] *Lives were taken in the air to save lives on the ground.*

The Langley-based pilots were 96 miles away, Marr says. In Cleveland, Delta Flight 1989 landed safely, but the NEADS crew wouldn't learn that until later.

What was going to happen next? Staff Sgt. Mark Jennings, NEADS tracking technician, remembers asking himself: "Was the fourth one the last one and would there be more? It made me sit back and say, 'Is the world falling apart on us?' It was scary and there was a real feeling of uncertainty."

Marr began thinking out loud: "I turned to the staff and said, 'What more can we do? Let's get everyone in the air and see what they can provide us.' "

They needed help and literally went down the list calling every regular Air Force and Air National Guard unit in the northeast. "We just started opening our phone rosters and were trying to figure out which different Air Force units there were in the interior of the United States," Deskins says. "And we called these units individually to see if they could get planes up."

And it wasn't happening like it normally would, she says. Enlisted personnel were calling colonels directly, asking for their help. Rank didn't matter and virtually everyone would commit to getting fighters airborne. "It was unbelievable," says Tech. Sgt. Michael Cavalier, NEADS senior director technician. "There were Guard units I'd never heard of calling us asking how they could help. And we said, 'Yes, take off.' "

Canadian Forces Capt. Brian Nagel, who was chief of NEADS live exercises, says "guys were getting airborne from a news report and phone call from us."

"I called up one unit and the guy says, 'Who are you and what do you want?' " Nagel recalls. "I

told him to go watch CNN and that I'd phone him back. So I phone him back and he says, 'Here's what we've got and here's what we can do for you.' "

As Col. Robert Knauff, commander of the 174th Fighter Wing in Syracuse, told Marr: "Give us 10 minutes, we can arm up guns; give us 30 minutes, we can put heat-seekers on the wings; give us an hour, and we'll put radar missiles on board." The first two Syracuse-based F-16s were up by 10:44 a.m. [15] Two more fighters were up a few minutes later, but there was no time to load missiles on any of them. The pilots' mission was vague, but they believed an airliner was heading toward Washington, D.C.

"Our pilots were told to get in the air and get

Photo by Master Sgt. Tom Louis, 177th Fighter Wing, New Jersey Air National Guard

Security Forces Senior Airman Raynaldo Baez of the New Jersey Air National Guard 177th Fighter Wing stands guard on the flight line Sept. 15, 2001.

Photo by Master Sgt. Don Taggart, 177th Fighter Wing, New Jersey Air National Guard

From left, New Jersey Air National Guardsmen Senior Airman James Keefe, Airman 1st Class Frank Dolcemascolo and Staff Sgt. Richard Johnson, 177th Fighter Wing weapons load crew members, raise an AIM-120A using an MJ1 bomb lift "Jammer." The missile was loaded onto an F-16 for an Operation Noble Eagle mission.

their tasking from NEADS once airborne," says Col. Tony Basile, 174th Fighter Wing vice commander. "The first two airborne were trying to intercept the flight that crashed in Pennsylvania but that airplane had actually hit the ground. ... There were several others NEADS wasn't sure of, so our mission was to intercept those airplanes."

The Ohio Air National Guard 180th Fighter Wing was the first unit outside the East Coast to answer the sector's plea. Controllers notified the wing at 10:01 a.m.; several armed F-16s departed Toledo Express Airport at 10:17 a.m., according to wing records.

Jets from the 177th Fighter Wing, New Jersey Air National Guard, were airborne within an hour after the Pentagon attack, says Col. Mike Cosby, wing commander. And the F-16s were fully loaded.

"The mind-set a lot of old military guys have is

that the Guard is the standby force," Marr says. "But these Guard guys got up very, very quickly."

As pilots and aircrews throughout the country went to battle, historic events were taking place at the highest levels.

"As this is all transpiring extraordinarily rapidly ... some five minutes after United Flight 93 crashed in Pennsylvania, President George W. Bush, through Vice President Dick Cheney, gave authority to shoot down civilian airplanes that looked like they were going to be used as fuel-air bombs," Arnold says. "I have the authority in case of an emergency to declare a target hostile and shoot it down under an emergency condition ... but it was comforting to know we legally had the authority from the president of the United States."

The order would go even further in Washington, D.C., where local airspace was declared a "weapons-free" zone. [16] Fighter pilots were given unparalleled orders to fire upon anything around the nation's capital that refused to respond to Air Traffic Control or NORAD direction.

"The president had declared Washington, D.C., and national capital region to be a free-fire zone," Arnold says. "That is very unprecedented. It meant if a pilot saw an airplane within a 30-mile radius of Washington, D.C., and couldn't determine if it was a doctor flying back to his hometown, that pilot was not only allowed to, but expected to shoot that airplane down."

Some F-16 pilots from the 113th Wing, District of Columbia Air National Guard, were prepared to do it. They weren't in communication with NEADS that morning but knew their home city was in trouble. The wing, at Andrews Air Force Base, Md., is not part of the NORAD air sovereignty force and did not have an alert mission. But that did not stop pilots there from taking off to protect Washington, D.C., just miles from their own flight line.

Weapons-free zone

As the twin towers were burning live on CNN, weapons officer Maj. Dan Caine was worried. Not only was the country under terrorist attack, but three of the 113th Wing's F-16 pilots had not returned from a training mission. As the "SOF" — Supervisor of Flying — that morning, Caine was responsible for seeing those jets return safely to base.

"I called the Andrews tower and asked them if any Air Traffic Control measures were starting to go into effect with an eye toward the recovery of our airplanes," Caine says. "They indicated there was not and I called our contact at the Secret Service. He told me he wasn't sure, but that things were happening and he'd call me back. It was a very quick, confusing conversation."

Andrews is home to Air Force One, and 113th Wing pilots are used to working with the Secret Service, but "weren't thinking about defending anything," says Lt. Col. Marc Sasseville, commander of the wing's 121st Fighter Squadron. "Our primary concern was what would happen with the air

Photo by Tech. Sgt. Corensa Brooks, 113th Wing, District of Columbia Air National Guard

Photos by Tech. Sgt. Corensa Brooks, 113th Wing, District of Columbia Air National Guard

Above: Weapons load crew members from the 113th Wing, District of Columbia Air National Guard, work feverishly to arm an F-16 for a mission over Washington, D.C., on Sept. 11, 2001.

Left: District of Columbia Air National Guardsman Master Sgt. Steve Proctor, 113th Wing aircraft generation squadron, loads bullets onto an F-16.

Opposite page: The weapons are driven across Andrews Air Force Base, Md., for delivery to the flight line on Sept. 11.

Above: District of Columbia Air National Guardsmen Lt. Col. Marc Sasseville, 113th Wing F-16 pilot, and Senior Master Sgt. Jackie Dade, 113th Wing aircraft generation squadron flight chief, discuss the mission prior to takeoff on Sept. 11, 2001.

Right: An F-16 maintainer from the 113th Wing directs a jet on the runway at Andrews Air Force Base, Md., on Sept. 11, 2001.

traffic system." [17]

But the Secret Service would soon call back: "(The agent) asked, 'Can you get airplanes up?'" Caine recalls. "Then he told us to stand by and that somebody else would call. When I heard the tone in his voice, I called our bomb dump and told them to uncrate our missiles."

On the opposite side of Andrews Air Force Base, the 113th Wing munitions crew began unloading bullets and AIM-9 "Sidewinders" from storage sheds. "There were six of us there and we had 28 missiles to unload, and they each have three components" says Senior Master Sgt. David Bowman, 113th Wing munitions supervisor. "And if you

drop one, you can't use it anymore. We were doing it as fast as we could, because for all we knew the terrorists were getting ready to hit us."

As the crew carefully but quickly loaded the weapons onto a flatbed trailer, the phone was ringing again at the squadron operations desk. Caine answered a phone call from someone in the White House requesting armed fighters over Washington. "I could hear plain as day the vice president talking in the background," Caine says. "That's basically where we got the execute order. It was 'VFR (Visual Flight Rules) direct.'

"I handed the phone to my commander and said, 'I'm going to go fly.'"

　　　　　　　　　　　　　　　　　　　　AIR WAR OVER AMERICA

Brig. Gen. David Wherley Jr., 113th Wing commander, had just arrived at the operations desk. He would find himself on several phone calls that morning, desperately seeking airborne authorization for his fighters. "I dial the White House JOC (Joint Operations Center) and the news is showing the White House with people running out the front door," Wherley says. "And the phone rings about eight times before somebody picks up and ... they have nobody in uniform, it was all Secret Service people and a team communicating with the president."

A woman at the JOC — the Secret Service command and control center — answered the phone. "I'm thinking these are civilians and they don't deal in the language of the military, the rules of engagement, so I asked her, 'What do they want me to do?'" he recalls. "She was standing next to the vice president (Dick Cheney) and she said, 'They want you to put a CAP up.'

"Basically what they told me, and this is another one of those things that's clear in my mind ... 'We want you to intercept any airplane that attempts to fly closer than 20 miles around any airport around the Washington area. ... Attempt to turn them away, do whatever you can to turn them away and if they won't turn away use whatever force is necessary ... to keep them from hitting a building downtown.'"

Everything was happening at once, says wing safety officer Lt. Col. Phil Thompson, who was now the acting SOF. "We were taking calls from the Secret Service and Washington Center," he recalls. "We have a special relationship with the Secret Service and know these guys by name and face. ... They were worried about Flight 93."

In the 113th Wing intelligence office, Maj. David McNulty and Senior Airman Juan Garcia were hurriedly calling every agency from the CIA to FBI to FAA to authenticate the flood of information. "I even called the National Security Agency 24-hour information desk and they knew nothing more than I did," McNulty says. "We were all getting our information from CNN. But the White House JOC told me eight planes were unaccounted for."

Three wing F-16s, meanwhile, were still airborne. "We had gone up to (the gunnery range in) Dare County, North Carolina, to drop some bombs and hit a refueling tanker and come on back," says flight lead Maj. Billy Hutchison. "It was going to be an uneventful day. It was actually a beautiful day."

"We're about halfway back when I am able to talk to the SOF, Lt. Col. Phil Thompson, who is at the desk with Brigadier General Wherley," he says. "Because they've seen what has happened on TV, they tell me to return to base 'buster'; buster means as fast as the aircraft will fly. So we light afterburners and we are coming back at Mach as quick as we can get back. ... As I get back, I cross the Potomac River on the south end of Maryland and Virginia, and I see a big column of smoke. It was so clear and there was no haze in the air. I tell the SOF, 'It looks like there's been an explosion near (Ronald Reagan Washington) National Airport. What's going on?'"

"He said, 'We know. Just keep coming.'"

As Hutchison approached the runway to touch down, Thompson and Wherley inquired over the radio about the trio's fuel status. Nobody had enough gas, but Hutchison had the most. Although he was at 2,800 pounds — like one-eighth a tank in your car — Wherley told him to take off again.

Department of Defense photo by Tech. Sgt. Cedric H. Rudisill

An aerial view Sept. 14, 2001, of the destruction caused when a hijacked commercial jetliner crashed into the Pentagon on Sept 11, 2001.

"I was given information to intercept an aircraft coming toward D.C. and prevent it from reaching D.C.," Hutchison says.

"We had something coming down the Potomac at low altitude," Thompson says. "Brigadier General Wherley is standing here and we've got the tower with the Secret Service agent and they want us to launch anything we've got. And the general said, 'Do it.'"

Hutchison taxied at high speed down the runway and took off at 10:33 a.m. [18] "I was already cleared through tower, who is listening to Washington Approach frantic with what they seem to think are aircraft coming their way. ... There is another aircraft, and it's United Flight 93. They don't know what's going on, but only know the direction it's coming and apparently have been given information that it's coming their way."

In reality, United Airlines Flight 93 had crashed 30 minutes earlier, but in the haze and fog of war that tragic day, that information was unavailable. Hutchison continued looking for the plane. "I took off without afterburner to conserve fuel, go across the White House over the Georgetown area and continue northwest up the Potomac," he says.

When Hutchison reached the northern part of the river near Frederick, Md., controllers at Washington Center asked him to change course. "They asked me to turn to D.C. and all the while my gas is depleting," he says. "And I don't have live bullets, just training rounds."

"I terminate the intercept and come back to D.C.," Hutchison says. "Washington Center is still vectoring me around trying to pick up potential threats to the area which happened to be helicopters actually responding to the Pentagon scene. All the while, when I took off from Andrews, I could see what was going on over the Pentagon because I was so low. But it wasn't until I actually flew past it that I actually saw it was the Pentagon. I circled at a couple of hundred feet at the most just to, one, investigate, and two, give the people on the ground some semblance of security of an American fighter coming by. And apparently it changed the mood for a lot of people when they saw that.

"After that point, I'm emergency fuel, the lowest I've ever been in an F-16, and tell Washington Center I must leave and they say I'm cleared to return to base and that two more aircraft are coming out of Andrews."

❑❑❑

Sasseville and Capt. Heather Penney were on their way. Before they stepped to the jets, Wherley made very clear what they might have to do: "My translation of the rules to 'Sass' was, 'You have weapons-free flight-lead control,'" Wherley says. "I said, 'Do you understand what I'm asking you to do?'

"And they both said: 'Yes.'"

"And I told them to be careful. It was important for them to understand that this was weapons-free."

Weapons loaders on the ramp were working feverishly to arm missiles, but there was no time. Sasseville and Penney took off from Andrews at 10:42 a.m. [19] Their planes were loaded with 20mm training rounds, hardly enough to bring down an airliner, they concede. "Sass looked at me and his eyes were just burning," says Penney, a rookie pilot and lieutenant at the time. "We were running to the jets and jumped in our airplanes and we didn't even have a full load on the guns. I'd never scrambled before, I'd never done this."

"I was screaming to the maintainers to pull the chocks and the guys were pulling the pins to arm the guns," she recalls. "We were going without INS (Inertial Navigation System)."

The two were in their jets watching Hutchison take off before them and listening to scants of in-formation on their radio frequencies. "I don't have the whole picture, but have word from Washington National Approach that something is coming," Sasseville says. "We had hot guns, but only training bullets. ... I'm thinking, 'Wow, we're in a little trouble here.'"

Penney and Sasseville would fly at low altitudes over the capital, Pentagon burning in the distance, unaware the North Dakota pilots were hovering around 20,000 feet. The North Dakota pilots were communicating with controllers at NEADS; the Washington, D.C., pilots with civilian controllers at the FAA. The pilots were on different radio frequencies, but would all hear remarkable words on a shared channel: *"Attention all aircraft monitoring Andrews tower frequency. Andrews and Class Bravo airspace is closed. No general aviation aircraft are permitted to enter Class Bravo airspace. Any infractions will be shot down."* [20]

"When we took off I hadn't even thought about how I would down an airplane," Penney says. "Later I'm thinking, 'I only have 100 bullets. What am I going to do?'"

"I could make one pass with the gun, maybe I could scrape my gear on the wing, but it didn't hit me until two weeks later that's what they expected us to do. ... I was in war mode; the emotional element wasn't relevant to what I had to do."

Sasseville, an airline pilot on a military leave of absence, also thought about how he might bring down an airliner, and says it was a scary proposition. "We're talking about shooting down a U.S. air carrier with Americans on board, the whole gamut, women and children," he says. "We had no real weapons and we didn't have a whole lot of options. Once you make that decision, how are you going to do that with the limited ordnance you have? In combat, as long as you can disable an airplane, depending on your role, you've done your job."

"I was going into this moral or ethical justification of the needs of the many to the needs of the few," he says. "The passengers on United Flight 93 went through that same thing. They made the

Airplanes line the runway of Halifax International Airport, Nova Scotia, after being diverted there Sept. 11, 2001. More than 7,000 passengers were affected.

Photo by Steve Emmons

Photo courtesy of Halifax International Airport Authority

9.11.01

decision we didn't have to make."

With minds racing, Sasseville and Penney continued flying and say they found an aerial ghost town over the normally busy Washington, D.C. Two more 113th Wing F-16 pilots, Caine and Capt. Brandon Rasmussen, would take off a few minutes after them, but their jets would each be armed with hot guns and two AIM-9 Sidewinder missiles.

Chief Master Sgt. Roy Belknap, 113th Wing production superintendent, watched in amazement as crews loaded live ordnance with pilots in the cockpits. "That's the first time that has ever happened here," the 33-year veteran says. "Our guys were hanging live AIM-9s with aircrews in airplanes waiting for us to get done so they could crank and go. What they did was unprecedented."

By the book, it takes three hours to bring weapons from storage sheds and load them on the jets, but on Sept. 11, 2001, it took the 113th Wing weapons crews 45 minutes, Belknap says.

Rasmussen says his adrenaline level was high as he took off toward the great unknown. "Once maintenance armed us up, we took off," he says. "I had never flown with real missiles and had never so much as seen them on the jet."

"We take to the air and are talking to Washington Center on the radio and we're used to working with AWACS (Airborne Warning and Control System) weapons controllers or GCI (Ground Control Intercept). ... We knew NORAD had implemented SCATANA and three things have already been hit when we get up in the air. So we're trying to identify people who are not talking to Air

Traffic Control. ... We probably intercepted five to 10 aircraft apiece."

Although they were in weapons-free airspace, none of the pilots believed anything they encountered was enough of a threat to actually shoot, but "quite a few people got scared out of the air," Rasmussen says. "On that day, we owned the universe over D.C. at any altitude, any location, as long as it was in the interest of protecting the capital."

Adds Caine, "Certainly there were times when rules of engagement triggers were met, but not executed and thankfully so. Cooler heads prevailed or it could have been an even uglier day than it was."

In efforts to clear the skies above Washington, Happy Hooligan F-16 pilots Eckmann and Derrig were directed to intercept some low-altitude unknowns. Those "unknowns" were their military brethren from the District of Columbia Air National Guard.

"Air Traffic Control had started turning everyone away from Washington, D.C.," Eckmann says. "Normally it's a pretty busy area and we were getting vectored on people who weren't obeying that. We got vectored on the D.C. guys taking off out of Andrews ... the military knew they were taking off but Air Traffic Control didn't realize they were military."

The 113th Wing pilots "started in a low Combat Air Patrol and didn't even know we were there," Eckmann says. "They did a fantastic job getting there in the amount of time they did. That was great, considering they weren't on alert. I know how much time it takes to put missiles on planes, and they were fast."

Soon the pilots would all end up on the same frequency. "About halfway through our sortie, we learned about three other F-16s that had been airborne a lot longer than we had," Sasseville says. "We were all airborne at the same time but nobody knew it."

As Sasseville was commanding the low-altitude

Secretary of Defense Donald Rumsfeld conducts the first Pentagon briefing after the terrorist attack there Sept. 11, 2001. He is joined by Gen. Henry H. Shelton, who was chairman of the Joint Chiefs of Staff, since retired, and Sen. John Warner, Virginia.

CAP, the Happy Hooligans commanded their own CAP several thousand feet above. "At first a low CAP and high-altitude CAP emerged," Eckmann says. "It took awhile before we were all talking on the same radio. We had two different units here and two different things going on. I had set up a racetrack CAP and he (Sasseville) had set up a tactical CAP.

"We eventually said, 'Here's what we're going to do, we'll take care of the high CAP and you guys take care of the low CAP.' As it progressed ... planes started moving up for fuel conservation and soon the lowest CAP altitude was 10,000 feet, but at that time we had everything cleared."

Essential AWACS and refueling aircraft would arrive sent by the CONR and NEADS leaders.

With a good radar picture and enough fuel, Sasseville and the other pilots used Ronald Reagan Washington National Airport as their "bull's-eye." By dividing the airspace into four sections, they could better communicate with the FAA about the locations of unknown aircraft. Virtually every pilot who flew that day has nothing but praise for FAA controllers who quickly learned to speak the language of the military.

"Nobody had trained to do this," Sasseville says. "But everybody pitched in to make it happen. Everybody was doing smart, safe things, from operations crews to the maintainers setting up airplanes and loading live AMRAAMs (Advanced Medium Range Air-to-Air Missiles)."

Gen. John Jumper, Air Force chief of staff, would

White House photo by Eric Draper

After departing Offutt Air Force Base, Neb., President George W. Bush confers with Vice President Dick Cheney from Air Force One during his flight to Andrews Air Force Base, Md., Sept. 11, 2001. The president's aircraft was escorted by armed fighter jets, including F-16s from the 147th Fighter Wing, Texas Air National Guard. The president was a member of the Houston-area unit in the early 1970s.

later reflect: "The events of 11 September were an imponderable, unknowable circumstance. We performed magnificently."[21]

Eberhart, NORAD commander, concurs: "I will always believe there would have been other attacks had we not grounded airplanes and got the fighters airborne."[22]

Guarding the president

As Air National Guard pilots were flying CAPs above Washington, D.C., President Bush was departing Sarasota, Fla., on Air Force One. Arnold

and his staff at the CONR Air Operations Center were coordinating the president's movement and scrambling fighters to keep him safe. All the while, reported hijackings were rampant.

"An AWACS was flying a training mission off the coast of Florida," Arnold recalls. "President Bush was in Sarasota and we moved the AWACS toward the president. Then we received tasking from the Secret Service through the Joint Staff and NORAD to follow the president and protect him."[23]

Months earlier, Arnold had made arrangements with Brig. Gen. Ben Robinson, then-commander of the 552nd Air Control Wing at Tinker Air Force Base, Okla., for AWACS support during exercises

AIR WAR OVER AMERICA

simulating attacks on the United States. Now the AWACS would be flown in a real-world scenario that only hours before was unimaginable.

"The AWACS pilot thought it was an exercise and we then told him what happened at the World Trade Center," Arnold says. "He realized his responsibility was to follow the president. We told him to follow Air Force One and he asked the question we all asked: 'Where is it going?' We said, 'We can't tell you. Just follow it.'"

The Southeast Air Defense Sector — SEADS — put pilots from the Minnesota Air National Guard 148th Fighter Wing at Tyndall Air Force Base on battle stations. Pilots sat in their cockpits awaiting word to go, but Air Force One moved so quickly they were never scrambled. Alert fighters from Ellington Field, Texas, were scrambled instead. Four F-16s from the 147th Fighter Wing, Texas Air National Guard, escorted President Bush from the panhandle of Florida to Barksdale Air Force Base, La. The president was being escorted by some of his own — he flew F-102 interceptors for the Houston-area unit in the early 1970s.

By the time the president landed at Barksdale, the Louisiana Air National Guard 159th Fighter Wing, New Orleans, already had four of its F-15s loaded with live missiles. The unit, not normally part of the NORAD alert system, was scrambled by SEADS about the same time the president was leaving the base. "As we were all watching the news, the wing leadership decided to configure our jets and get ready," says Maj. Jeff Woelbling, 122nd Fighter Squadron weapons officer. "Our weapons guys were hustling to get missiles on the rails. When I got to the jet, the maintainer told me he needed five more minutes. I said, 'You've got three.' He did it in about a minute and a half."

Nobody knew where the president was headed. "When Air Force One took off out of Barksdale, we were scrambled because SEADS didn't know his route of flight," says Lt. Col. Randy Riccardi, who was the 122nd Fighter Squadron commander at the time. "We were in a four-ship and turned

north toward Barksdale and the president was already airborne. We were 300 miles behind him since SEADS didn't know where he was going."

"It wasn't until the president was near Offutt (Air Force Base, Neb.), that we turned around and came back," Riccardi says. "That was about a 90-minute mission and later, at about 5:15, we were scrambled again."

"We ended up flying a six-hour and 15-minute mission over Houston that night," Riccardi says.

The response in Louisiana that day was indicative of the quick reactions across the Air National Guard map. The military's homeland defense mission was just beginning.

Somewhere in the southern skies was Air Force One, having left Barksdale for an undisclosed location. "When we left Barksdale we didn't know where we were going," says Maj. Shane Brotherton, a Texas Air National Guard F-16 pilot who escorted the president's plane that morning. "We were actually about to run out of gas when a SEADS controller told us a tanker was on its way. We were flying north two miles directly behind Air Force One and didn't know where we'd be landing. They wouldn't tell us, so we just kept getting more gas."

By the time Air Force One landed at Offutt Air Force Base, the F-16s were so heavy from refueling that the pilots had to burn off gas before they could land, Brotherton says. Once on the ground, they had a meeting with the pilot of Air Force One, who asked them about the capabilities of the F-16. The Air Force One aircraft commander couldn't tell them where they were going next, so the F-16 pilots couldn't file a flight plan. They got a candy bar and soda instead.

As the pilots were waiting, President Bush and his team were joining the air threat conference call. By this time, Arnold and Marr were also on the line.

"We were watching potentially hijacked aircraft," Arnold says. "I'm on the phone listening to the president talk to the secretary of defense and they were concerned about an aircraft that had taken off from Madrid and was going to land at John F. Kennedy International. ... We didn't know where that plane was. About that time, Bob Marr calls me, who was also on the conference call, but called me directly and said, 'We just talked to the airline and that aircraft is back on the ground in Madrid.' "

"I picked up the hot line and said, 'Mr. President, this is the CONR commander. ... No problem with Madrid.' It was valid information and the president said, 'OK, then I'm getting airborne.' "

The F-16 pilots there to escort the president were still waiting word to go. "The Air Force One pilot had gotten our cell phone numbers and said he'd call us when we'd be leaving," Brotherton says. "We were eating our snacks and heard jet noise. It was Air Force One and they'd never called us. We got to the jets and he's taxiing fast and never stopped. Now we're taxiing fast and we blast off. By the time we got airborne, he was 100 miles in front of us. ... Air Force One is fast but you wouldn't think so. But it can move. There were some Sioux City guys (Iowa Air National Guard) up there but the Air Force One pilot told them he'd had the Texas boys with him from the start. All across the country we were playing catch up, because he was moving. And we didn't catch up until we were nearing Washington."

As the president's 747 was approaching Andrews Air Force Base, the North Dakota and District of Columbia pilots were still flying CAPs over the city. A number of fighter jets from across the northeast had joined them. "It was like someone kicked a hornet's nest," one pilot remembers.

Soon the FAA would report an aircraft racing toward Air Force One. Fighter jets quickly intercepted the unknown, a Lear business jet in the wrong place at the wrong time. Air Force One touched down safely at Andrews, surrounded by

armed fighter escorts. The president boarded his Marine One helicopter and arrived at the White House around 7 p.m.

The airplane that had landed in Madrid was the last possible hijacking in the air that day.

From his radar scope, NEADS Master Sgt. Joe McCain believes he saw American Airlines Flight 11 disappear over New York on Sept. 11, 2001. It was 8:46 a.m. Eastern Standard Time, a tragic tick of the clock that forever

Two F-16 fighters assigned to the Texas Air National Guard 147th Fighter Wing are armed and ready to respond to unknown threats. Pilots from the Houston-area unit escorted Air Force One across the country Sept. 11, 2001.

Photo by Lans Stout for Code One magazine

seared itself into the American psyche. It was the unforgettable moment when the first of hundreds of innocent victims were killed that day. Twelve hours later, after a day that seemed like an eternity yet flew by remarkably fast, Joe McCain was home with his family.

"I have three kids and my youngest is 8," McCain says. "I'm sitting there at the kitchen table taking off my boots. It's the worst day I've ever had in the service and my son asks, 'Daddy, are they going to get us?' I told him he was safe, but the next few days I'd be gone a lot.

"That's what brought it home for me."

1 Northeast Air Defense Sector, transcript of recorded phone conversations between the sector and Federal Aviation Administration, 11 September 2001, n.p.

2 Larry K. Arnold, telephone interview with author, 25 July 2002.

3 William A. Scott, 2001. *Operation Noble Eagle: September 11, 2001, Air War Over America.* Panama City, Fla.: Microsoft PowerPoint presentation.

4 H. Darr Beiser, "Amid terror, a drastic decision: Clear the skies," *USA Today* online, 16 August 2002, n.p.

5 Hart Seely, "They scrambled jets, but it was a race they could not win," *The (Syracuse, N.Y.) Post-Standard*, 20 January 2002, sec. 1A, p. 6.

6 Ibid., p. 6.

7 William B. Scott, "Exercise Jump-Starts Response to Attacks," *Aviation Week & Space Technology*, June 3, 2002, 48.

8 Beiser, n.p.

9 Northeast Air Defense Sector, transcript, n.p.

10 Robert Marr, 2001. *America Under Attack: 11 Sep 01.* Rome, N.Y.: Microsoft PowerPoint presentation; Dean Eckmann, telephone interview with author, 6 December 2002.

11 Eckmann, telephone interview with author.

12 Tim Duffy, telephone interview with author, 22 October 2002.

13 Scott, "Exercise Jump-Starts Response to Attacks," 48.

14 Robert Marr, interview with author, 25 June 2002.

15 Robert Marr, 2001. *America Under Attack: 11 Sep 01.*

16 Larry K. Arnold, telephone interview with author, 27 November 2002.

17 William B. Scott, "F-16 Pilots Considered Ramming Flight 93," *Aviation Week & Space Technology,* September 9, 2002, 7.

18 David F. Wherley Jr., 113th Wing operations desk records of 11 September 2001.

19 Ibid.

20 Heather Penney, interview with author, 18 September 2002; recording from cockpit provided to William A. Scott by David F. Wherley Jr.

21 William A. Scott, conversation with author, 16 December 2002, said in a speech by Gen. John Jumper at 2002 CSAF Doctrine Summit, Maxwell Air Force Base, Ala., 10 December 2002.

22 Ralph E. Eberhart, press conference at Tyndall Air Force Base, Fla., 1 August 2002.

23 Eric Hehs, "Major General Larry Arnold, Commander, 1st Air Force, Tyndall Air Force Base, Florida," *Code One, Lockheed Martin Aeronautics Company,* First Quarter 2002, 6.

With smoke still rising from Ground Zero, the Statue of Liberty was a warm sight for sailors aboard the USNS Comfort as they transited the Hudson for relief efforts.

9.11.01

CHAPTER 4

THE NOBLE EAGLE FLIES:
Threat suddenly changes

Air defense new priority as terrorists turn airliners into weapons of war

The images that kept Maj. Gen. Larry K. Arnold awake at night were like eerie plots in a sci-fi horror film: cruise missiles, nukes, biological warfare, chemicals, and airplanes in the hands of terrorists.

"I lie awake worrying," Arnold told The Associated Press in early 2000. "It is one thing to put a truck inside the twin trade towers and blow it up. It is quite another to be able to fly a weapon across our borders. That is an attack, a direct attack, an unambiguous attack from outside our country." [1]

Then Sept. 11 happened, a twisted nightmare far scarier than Arnold ever could have imagined. With a Cold War mentality that the demons would come from outside America's shores, Arnold and his staff were blindsided when the fear struck from within. "No, we did not envision people hijacking airplanes from within the United States, taking over those aircraft and using them as fuel-air bombs," says the retired commander of 1st Air Force and the Continental United States North American Aerospace Defense Command Region. "As much as you brief what could happen in the future, I think from an intellectual standpoint, we realized the

Minnesota Air National Guard F-16s assigned to the 148th Fighter Wing fly Combat Air Patrol missions over Washington, D.C., in support of Operation Noble Eagle.

Photos by Master Sgt. Dean Kuhlman, 148th Fighter Wing, Minnesota Air National Guard

greatest threat to the United States prior to Sept. 11, 2001, was going to be a terrorist attack. But I did not envision that it would be hijacked airplanes run into buildings like that."

In the world before Sept. 11, Arnold had visions of light aircraft sneaking across America's air borders to wage biological, chemical or nuclear attack. And he wasn't convinced the NORAD alert fighter force was big enough to stop it. The asymmetric threat — the small, unknown enemy preying upon the behemoth United States — was a nagging, constant worry. "That was our thought," Arnold says. "That is what our mission was about. Our mission was not about the internal threat."

"We thought an attack in the United States was a law enforcement issue, and it was, right up until Sept. 11."

The night of the attacks, 119th Fighter Wing pilot Capt. Craig Borgstrom descended his F-16 "Fighting Falcon" into Langley Air Force Base, Va., after hours of intercept missions over Washington, D.C. As he taxied his aircraft safely in, he still didn't know all that had happened in his country that day. But the scene through the jet canopy told him everything had changed.

"When we recovered into our alert facility, there were more missiles on our ramp than my eyes have ever seen," the North Dakota Air National Guardsman says. "At this point, I still had no idea about the airliners. I pulled into the alert barn and there were load teams with missiles and trailers everywhere. I talked to the crew chief and my first question was, 'What else did they get?' He wasn't sure, but thought there were others at that point. I knew a really terrible thing had happened."

There was a new threat now: It was on the inside and sent America's air sovereignty mission reeling.

When Arnold went to sleep Sept. 10, 2001, he had 14 alert fighters on his watch, all dedicated to

protecting thousands of miles of American air borders. When Arnold finally went to sleep just before sunrise Sept. 12, America's air sovereignty force had been catapulted into a full-fledged air defense arsenal, with more than 400 alert fighters, Airborne Warning and Control System aircraft and tankers postured for battle. [2] The seven alert sites around the periphery of the continental United States grew ten times over to 69-plus sites scattered about the country. [3] Not even the Cuban Missile Crisis of 1962 saw such a build up of raw air power. [4] Within days, America's military had a new mission: Operation Noble Eagle. The Noble Eagle name encompasses U.S. military operations associated with homeland defense and civil support to federal, state and local agencies — air defense playing a major role. [5] More than 30 Air National Guard fighter wings and nearly two dozen refueling wings were immediately mobilized; President George W. Bush, meanwhile, approved the call up of up to 50,000 military reservists. [6]

Long-standing principles succumbed to the rapid response. A Civil War-era military code, the Posse Comitatus Act that prohibits federal troops from performing civil law enforcement duties, was waived at the highest levels. "Operation Noble Eagle operations were cleared of Posse Comitatus issues by the National Command Authorities," says retired Col. William A. Scott, 1st Air Force director of plans, programs and requirements. "The NCA directed this response because law enforcement agencies don't have the capabilities we have to deal with a hijacked airborne threat."

As for formal deployment orders, initially there were none. "The kinds of missions our people were flying were the kinds of missions you'd fly in defense of counterair in any theater deployed to, like Southern Watch or Northern Watch," Arnold says. "But our people weren't deployed anywhere."

Instead of Baghdad, airmen found themselves flying defensive patterns over their own cities and homes like San Francisco and Dallas, a radically different concept for the NORAD

A New York City firefighter pauses amid the devastation of the World Trade Center Sept. 15, 2001.

air sovereignty force. Suddenly, 1st Air Force and CONR were coordinating air defense operations within America and still maintaining the traditional look outward.

"Early on, which made things a lot simpler, Gen. (Ralph E.) Eberhart, the commander of NORAD, named me the Joint Force Air Component Commander," Arnold explains. "Along with that title, I was the Area Air Defense Commander and along with that the air control authority for the continental United States. ... If someone wanted to fly a plane, they had to come through us, when we the military, still had control of the airspace."

Essentially, Arnold was responsible for "anything that flew in the United States," he says, and could order a civilian airliner shot down by one of his own. It was a tall order, but Arnold is a tall man.

Guarding the homeland

In the immediate wake of Sept. 11, civilian aviation was brought to a historic standstill. Hundreds of planes were packed like sardines on Canadian runways in Newfoundland and Nova Scotia.

For several weeks, NORAD and the joint Department of Defense and Federal Aviation Administration Air Traffic Services Cell served as the hub of all government and civilian air traffic in the United States. [7] In that dramatic twist to NORAD's traditional mission, scores of fighters, tankers and surveillance aircraft were flying both planned and random Combat Air Patrols across the nation and

Petty Officer 3rd Class Edmond Scott directs an E-2C "Hawkeye" from Airborne Early Warning Squadron 125 into launch position on the flight deck of the USS George Washington (CVN 73), Sept. 13, 2001. The Norfolk, Va.-based ship was providing air defense to New York City while waiting for tasking from NORAD.

U.S. Navy photo by Petty Officer 3rd Class J. Scott Campbell

Photo by Senior Airman Brett R. Ewald, 148th Fighter Wing, Minne

round-the-clock sorties over New York and Washington, D.C. Instead of 14 jets, more than 100 fighters were on alert at 30 bases around the country. [8] Just as many tankers and AWACS were available to counter the domestic air threat. [9]

For F-15 pilots Majs. Robert Martyn and Martin Richard, Operation Noble Eagle began the day they saw the World Trade Center burn. The Massachusetts Air National Guardsmen were some of the first scrambled when hijackers took over the skies Sept. 11. Running to their "Eagles," they were fixated on what they just heard from the 102nd Fighter Wing intelligence officer: *There could be 20 more of these out there.*

The frantic scramble orders of Sept. 11 evolved into six months of nonstop patrols over cities; "National Special Security Events" like the 2002 Winter Olympics; and key infrastructure across the nation. Martyn, Richard and thousands of other airmen were suddenly and urgently defending their own country against an unknown, intangible aggressor. "We have basically drilled holes in the sky since that day," Martyn said a year after the attacks.

Operations at home bring a unique sense of responsibility. "On missions overseas, there's more of an individual, a personal threat to you," Martyn says. "If your motors quit, you're going to have a tough life in Iraq. And it's a team burden to the Air Force. Over the States, there's more the feeling you're a policeman. I'm not the one being threatened here. ... The threat is much higher to civilians and everyone else than it is to us. I feel more like I'm protecting my kid than myself. Ultimately, there is no threat to me flying around in an F-15. It's safer than driving around in my car, but Southwest Asia is not like that."

□□□

Homeland air defense wouldn't come without costs and presented new challenges for NORAD and its forces. Round-the-clock sorties and the support needed to fly them was stressing the jets, robbing pilots of crucial training and working maintenance troops overtime.

"Right after Sept. 11, and what became very obvious, was the operations tempo of our flying units," Arnold says. "We would have to persuade Air Combat Command and the rest of the Air Force to put Operation Noble Eagle into the Aerospace Expeditionary Forces."

The AEF Center cycles Air Force units through deployments like operations Northern and Southern Watch. "Prior to Sept. 11, we'd been unsuccessful in getting the AEF Center to be responsible for relieving our air defense units when they went overseas," Arnold says. "In the aftermath of Sept. 11, it became critical that we become a part of the AEF system. But it took awhile ... until about November, when we were able to persuade the Air Force there had to be relief, that these people could not do this."

Within the first five months of the operation, Noble Eagle sorties exceeded those flown over Afghanistan for Operation Enduring Freedom. [10] According to NORAD records, from September to December 2001, the command responded to 214 domestic aviation events in response to FAA requests. In 88 of those instances, alert fighters were scrambled; 126 others were diverted from Com-

Photo by Eric Hehs, Code One magazine

Above: Maj. Gen. Larry K. Arnold was commander of 1st Air Force and the Continental United States NORAD Region from December 1997 until August 2002. Following the Sept. 11 attacks, he directed Operation Noble Eagle forces and spearheaded major improvements in America's air defenses. He retired after 37 years of service.

Left: Senior Airman Adam Skadsberg, weapons loader, 148th Fighter Wing, Minnesota Air National Guard, uploads 20mm ammunition into the F-16 gun system as Tech. Sgt. Kent Larson stands by. Both airmen and hundreds of others from the unit were activated in support of Operation Noble Eagle.

Weapons load team members from the 177th Fighter Wing, New Jersey Air National Guard, load an AIM-120 on an F-16 Oct. 4, 2001, in support of Operation Noble Eagle. Tech. Sgt. Wendell Hunte operates the MJ1 "Jammer" bomb lift; Master Sgt. Frank Buzby and Senior Airman James Keefer attach the AIM-120 to the aircraft; Senior Airman Neil March performs gun maintenance inside the access panel; and Senior Airman Tina Chaffins waits to install the control surfaces on the AIM-120.

bat Air Patrols. In the same period a year earlier, NORAD scrambled or diverted fighters 21 times. [11]

The scrambles — and sometimes intercepts — have drawn their share of media attention. In the summer of 2002, controllers at the Western Air Defense Sector scrambled two Arizona Air National Guard F-16s toward a Cessna squawking a hijack frequency. [12] It turned out to be a rookie pilot who accidentally hit the wrong switch.

In another incident, the Washington-based sector scrambled Oregon Air National Guard F-15s when a pilot threatened to ram his small plane into the tallest building in Portland. [13] It happened to be the same day a movie was being filmed nearby.

"We scrambled F-15s from the 142nd Fighter Wing in Portland and the pilot saw explosions on the ground," says WADS Commander Col. John Cromwell. "He had a sickening feeling that he failed until he found out the explosions were coming from a movie set."

Commercial flights have been under extreme scrutiny since Sept. 11. "There was a bomb scare on a flight from Honolulu to Seattle," Cromwell says. "We scrambled F-15s to escort the plane over the Pacific into Seattle and it was an uneventful landing. ... If an F-15 or F-16 is on your wing, it's not always a bad thing. Our job is to provide that emergency escort and assist if necessary."

Senior Airman Daniel Hassler, left, and Airman 1st Class Edward Grandy, members of the New Jersey Air National Guard 177th Fighter Wing maintenance squadron, remove an oil filter from a jet engine Oct. 3, 2001. Extra maintenance was required after the Sept. 11 attacks.

An F-15 assigned to the 102nd Fighter Wing, Massachusetts Air National Guard, is refueled by a KC-135R assigned to the 157th Air Refueling Wing, New Hampshire Air National Guard, during an Operation Noble Eagle mission over New York in November 2001.

Photo by Tech. Sgt. Alan Beaulieu, 157th Air Refueling Wing, New Hampshire Air National Guard

AIR WAR OVER AMERICA

The air defense boom was hardest in the Northeast, Arnold says, where fighters were flying nonstop over New York and Washington, D.C. Maintenance troops were getting valuable operational training, but pilots were seeing their tactical skills wane.

"Training was just gone," says Massachusetts F-15 pilot Richard. "When you're flying the CAP (Combat Air Patrol), it's mostly flying circles and if you have an intercept there's about four minutes of adrenaline. ... This was a situation we certainly didn't anticipate. But we are a cohesive combat fighter squadron and that's how we made it work. We have maintenance guys who had to leave fairly lucrative civilian jobs in Boston and now have a two-hour commute to work. If people hadn't volunteered and seriously sacrificed, it never would have gotten done."

The sacrifices are felt military wide, but the reserve status of the National Guard means people leave their civilian jobs behind when called to duty. Throughout the ongoing operation, the military has provided assistance to federal agencies in many areas: medicine, engineering, security, military working dogs, logistics, and communications. [14] Operation Noble Eagle is more than CAPs: Guardsmen have been dispatched to the nation's airports, nuclear power plants, international borders, national parks, bridges, and more. Security forces have shouldered a heavy burden. Some 70 percent of Guard members were partially mobilized; the call up can last two years. [15]

"Family is first, your civilian job is second and your military job is third," says Col. Mike Cosby, commander of the 177th Fighter Wing, New Jersey Air National Guard. "People have sacrificed, not in the way the people in the World Trade Center or Pentagon did, but they have put their professional and personal lives on hold to come out here and serve the country and have done it with dis-

tinction. And the American people have recognized that."

In the days and months following the attacks, Atlantic City Air National Guard Base served as a home for several airmen protecting the Eastern skies.

"We hosted units from Houston, Albuquerque, (N.M.), Sioux City, (Iowa), and many more," Cosby says. "They bring pilots, airplanes and a limited number of maintainers and experts in the back shop (fighter wing repair facility), and we provide weather, base operations, intelligence, command post, and gas in the airplanes. They came right in here and rolled with the punches and did a fantastic job of supporting NORAD and the Noble Eagle mission."

Between Atlantic City's 177th Fighter Wing and other units deployed there, more than 1,200 sorties were flown from September 2001 until March 2002, for more than 4,480 hours of flying time, Cosby says. Atlantic City's fleet of F-16s, manufactured in 1983, saw a year's flying time in six months, he adds.

Across the alert force, the 24-hour combat sorties equated to crew rest and scheduling problems, no time for personal leave and 12-hour shifts. "There will be turbulent times between now and until we establish the new normal for America," Cosby said nine months into Operation Noble Eagle. "Everyone from the command posts, security forces to fire departments is doing a great job, but after awhile it has to get to you, working five to six days a week, 12 hours a day."

At various times during Noble Eagle, some 90

Air Force, Air National Guard and Air Force Reserve wings have been under NORAD command and control. [16] Canadian Forces and planes have provided assets for the operation along with U.S. Marine Corps flying squadrons and the U.S. Naval 3rd Fleet. [17]

That unwavering support began Sept. 11.

Col. Bob Marr, Northeast Air Defense Sector commander, says 81 Air Force and Air National Guard units helped secure the skies that day. "The Terre Haute guys (181st Fighter Wing, Ind.,) locked down their base as soon as the towers were hit and started loading missiles, anticipating someone would be calling for help, which we did," he says. "The Burlington guys (158th Fighter Wing, Vt.,) were some of the first in the air heading straight for New York as a unit that was familiar with the NORAD mission. People were launching jets in record time."

In the six days following the attacks, Air Guard pilots flew more than 600 fighter sorties. [18] A number of the aircrews had never performed in an air defense capacity. And many of the fighters were parked on bases that weren't equipped to store munitions — one of many details that had to be addressed.

"Bottom line, people handled this very well," Arnold says. "People know how to fly CAPs. The biggest problem was somehow personalizing this thing. Some of these units did not know us personally and it's difficult to resolve that. One of the things we eventually did was send some of our people to all the units that were pulling alert and flying CAPs for us around the country. They were a sight for sore eyes for those units. Those units were des-

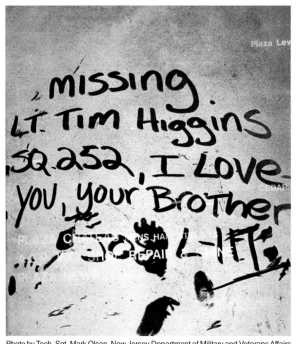

Photo by Tech. Sgt. Mark Olsen, New Jersey Department of Military and Veterans Affairs

perate to talk to somebody at 1st Air Force. People had questions. Alert facilities needed work and we were able to help by being an advocate for that."

At Selfridge Air National Guard Base, Mich., home of the 127th Wing, the local fire department vacated its building so F-16 aircrews had a place to sleep and work. Airmen had been sleeping in tents on the flight line for almost a month after Sept. 11. [19] "We can solve the lack of crew quarters in many different ways," Arnold says. "Some units have rented Winnebagos." [20]

Housing alert aircraft posed yet another problem, especially in cities with harsh winters. "Before Sept. 11 our mission was to train, so we could afford to let the snow melt before we flew," says retired Brig. Gen. Wayne L. Schultz, former commander of the Colorado Air National Guard 140th Wing near Denver. [21] An accelerated contract bid resulted in six temperature-moderated shelters to protect the F-16s and keep them in top shape for alert sorties. Even on the coldest days, deicing of aircraft will be unnecessary, improving response times. [22] At Andrews Air Force Base, Md., home of the 113th Wing, District of Columbia Air National Guard, five aircraft shelters were quickly built for the new F-16 alert commitment there. [23]

Modernizing a mission

Generating thousands of unprecedented combat flights over the continental United States was going to be a feat in and of itself. Since NORAD

Above: A chaplain counsels an Army National Guard member serving in New York City in late September 2001.

Left: Firefighters break from the destruction Sept. 14, 2001.

Opposite page: A brother reaches out through a dusty message as seen in this Sept. 14, 2001, photo. Firefighter Lt. Timothy Higgins, 43, was killed Sept. 11.

had always looked outward, its interior radar coverage was dismal. "Now we were suddenly looking in the interior of the country and didn't have the capability to do it," Arnold says.

Airborne surveillance was an immediate, yet partial, solution in the early days of the operation: Air Force E-3 AWACS, Navy E-2C "Hawkeyes" and U.S. Customs Service P-3s provided radar feeds to forces on the ground and in the air. [24] Navy Aegis cruisers also contributed to the new view inward. [25] But much more was needed to sustain effective 24-hour combat patrols over America. "We had three things to do," Arnold says. "We had to hook up radars so we could see the interior, had to have radios to talk to pilots and a command and control system capable of plugging in all those radars and radios ... so the air defense sectors could actually see and talk to our fighters."

The Air Force began revamping every facet of the mission as mandated at the highest levels of government and the Department of Defense. Air sovereignty fundamentals raced into the 21st century with Mach-like speed.

"We got better at everything we had to do, better at working with the Navy, better at scrambling and controlling airplanes and better with our radars," says Lt. Col. Clark "Buck" Rogers, deputy commander for operations at the Southeast Air Defense Sector, Tyndall Air Force Base, Fla. "The amount of change the air defense business went through is phenomenal. I don't think that in the history of the military you can find more rapid change in such a short period of time. It used to be months of funding and questions. We didn't have any of that. We said, 'You guys need to be on alert and the next thing you know, people are setting up tents and 'Winnebagos.'"

In the world before Sept. 11, America's long-range radars — Joint Surveillance System sites and tethered aerostats around the periphery of the country — were focused on planes coming toward the United States. Flights originating in the country and crossing the interior were automatically considered

U.S. Air Force photo by Staff Sgt. Michelle Leonard

AIR WAR OVER AMERICA

U.S. Air Force photo by Senior Airman Michele G. Misiano

Above: Weapons loaders from the Virginia Air National Guard 192nd Fighter Wing perform end of runway procedures before an F-16 takes off in support of Operation Noble Eagle on Oct. 30, 2001.

Left: Smoldering fires at the World Trade Center are reflected in the visor of a United States Air Force MH-53M helicopter flight engineer days after the Sept. 11 terrorist attack on the United States.

friendly. [26] And the dated NORAD Q-93 computers could not connect with the scores of FAA radars dotting the interior landscape.

"On Sept. 11, we were looking out — looking for the external threat," NORAD Commander Eberhart said months after the attacks. "We assumed anything in the United States was authorized to be there and did not constitute a threat. Tragically, we were wrong." [27]

One of the greatest technological advances in NORAD's 45-year history would come immediately on the heels of the terrorist attacks. [28] The "NORAD Contingency Suite," a computer software program purchased with $9 million in emergency response funds, would link NORAD with several interior FAA radars, giving controllers the capability to view more than 15,000 tracks at any moment per sector instead of 300 tracks before Sept. 11. [29]

"The beautiful map on the NORAD Contingency Suite enables us to see everything," says Maj. Sue Cheney, a WADS assistant flight commander. "We can see the airports, see where the planes take off and see the history of a track. We can look at a track and see if it took off in the United States."

The sharper view — in color on a graphics-intensive flat panel screen — is especially important in the West, where controllers keep a watchful eye on the Mexican border, she adds.

Cheney marvels at how quickly NORAD acquired the new technology. "In only a couple of months we were getting a whole new system installed," she says. "From the 11th of September, for the Air Force to buy and field a new system, that's just unbelievably quick. We'd done modernization for the better part of the decade and spent millions of dollars and got nothing. Two months after Sept. 11, we had a new system for a tiny fraction of that cost."

That rapid capability arose from a cruise missile defense "Advanced Concept Technology Demonstration" 1st Air Force had been conducting for more than a year — a prescient stroke of luck for NORAD and the United States.

Planning for war

Better radar pictures are just part of the story of how a mission changed overnight. Within a few days of the Sept. 11 attacks, the CONR Air Operations Center, run by the 701st Air Defense Squadron, would become a bona fide war machine.

The heart of Noble Eagle beats at the CONR AOC, the combat center in the continental United States dedicated to its defense. Much like a movie theater, only colder, the AOC is a typical air defense facility: dim, drab and windowless. It's where highly classified plans to protect the nation are born, approved and disseminated across NORAD. "Our command post, before Sept. 11, had 38 people that ran our AOC day to day," Arnold explains. "We eventually had 500 people running it." The first group of what would be more than 400 people arrived within nine days of the attacks, Scott says.

"The importance of the CONR Air Operations Center grew dramatically in the days following Sept. 11," says retired Col. Joe Kahoe, former 1st

Two F-16s assigned to the North Dakota Air National Guard 119th Fighter Wing fly a Combat Air Patrol mission over Washington, D.C., in support of Operation Noble Eagle.

Air Force and CONR assistant chief of operations. "We always thought we had an important role to play in defense of the homeland. In a matter of days, 1st Air Force and CONR received hundreds of thousands of dollars worth of computers and communications equipment that we had been struggling to obtain for years."

From the AOC comes the ATO —the Air Tasking Order — for a day's worth of Noble Eagle sorties. "Combat plans became a huge function," Arnold says. "We were used to writing a single ATO every week for all our alert prior to Sept. 11 and after Sept. 11, had to write an ATO every day that was larger than Northern Watch and Southern

Photo courtesy of 119th Fighter Wing, North Dakota Air National Guard

Grass roots efforts

High-visibility changes were everywhere as air defense was taking center stage across the terror-struck nation. The Department of Defense 2001 "Report of the Quadrennial Defense Review" would conclude: *"The highest priority of the U.S. military is to defend the Nation from all enemies."* [30] Grass roots efforts at the nation's air defense sectors were true to the cause.

Master Sgt. Jon Smith is the noncommissioned officer in charge of radio maintenance support at the Southeast Air Defense Sector. His wife gave birth to their first child in an emergency delivery Sept. 7, 2001. When the phone rang Sept. 11, they'd been home from the hospital one night, sleepless and unaware of the unfolding catastrophe.

"Col. (Dave) Webster (SEADS chief of communications and computer systems) asked me what it would take for us to install radios," Smith says. "I said, 'Sir, we can install radios wherever we need to as long as we can get telephone circuits.' "

Just a few days after the attacks, Smith and Master Sgt. Bruce Griswold, chief of computer maintenance, loaded up their equipment and headed to Dobbins Air Reserve Base in Georgia. Their mission: wire radios so ground controllers could communicate with fighter pilots flying over Atlanta.

"The point of the radios was to have connectivity," Smith explains. "The voice circuit and data circuit were routed back to Tyndall over telephone lines so the SEADS operators would have remote control of the radio. Now they could talk to the fighters for Combat Air Patrol missions."

Smith reported back to his boss. "I told Col. Webster we were looking good here and he said, 'Good work. The bad news is, I need you to get back ASAP for your day off with your wife and baby. When you get back, I'll tell you where you're going next.' "

The next stop was Louisiana. Then Texas —

Watch combined. This was not a small effort.

"Now you had combat plans people writing the ATO, had current operations people on the floor representing every specialty we had — command and control, AWACS, fighters, logistics. ... We had to have these people on duty. If there was a change to the ATO, we had to adjust the ATO and have the coordination for all of it to happen."

It was a tough, but attainable task, Arnold says: "I had confidence in our people. We trained daily, we conducted exercises and were inspected so we already knew our people were capable of doing the job. We knew how to run an AOC and how to obtain, allocate and apportion resources."

the president's ranch in Crawford needed protection. Then Arkansas. Another team installing the "radios on a stick," as crews dubbed them, went to North Carolina. Then Tennessee. Then Alabama.

"When you're in a crisis, you want people who can thrive without structure, who can just create it as they go along," says Col. Larry Kemp, SEADS commander.

For several weeks, Smith, Griswold and other SEADS specialists drove around the South, often getting supplies at the local Home Depot, so U.S. Air Force fighters could protect the country. "We had great support wherever we went," Smith says. "People bent over backward helping us out."

Hundreds of miles away at the Northeast Air Defense Sector, airspace specialists initiated an unprecedented 24-hour telephone bridge between the military and FAA. The crucial communication link began Sept. 11 and has been up ever since.

"It took about two seconds to realize that how we operated before Sept. 11 was not going to work," says Bill Ayers, Department of Defense airspace manager for NEADS. "We couldn't get the

Lisa Beamer, whose husband Todd Beamer was killed on United Airlines Flight 93, attends a dedication ceremony March 25, 2002, in Egg Harbor Township, N.J., headquarters of the New Jersey Air National Guard 177th Fighter Wing. A decal depicting Todd Beamer's inspiring words is displayed on Wing Commander Col. Mike Cosby's F-16. The phrase "Let's Roll" has come to represent the heroic spirit of those killed in the Sept. 11 terrorist attacks.

Photo by Senior Airman Andrew J. Merlock Jr., 177th Fighter Wing, New Jersey Air National Guard

THE NOBLE EAGLE FLIES

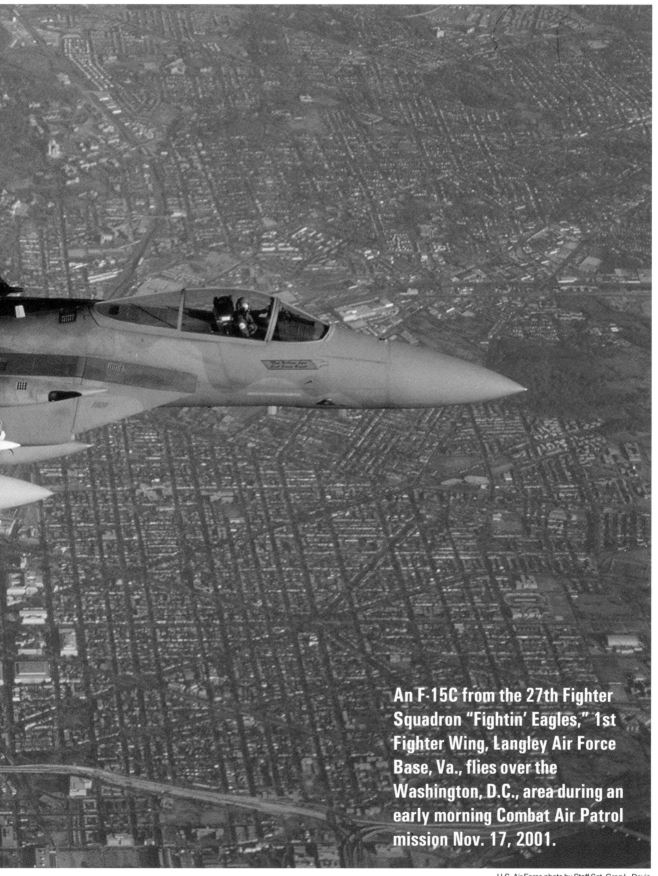

An F-15C from the 27th Fighter Squadron "Fightin' Eagles," 1st Fighter Wing, Langley Air Force Base, Va., flies over the Washington, D.C., area during an early morning Combat Air Patrol mission Nov. 17, 2001.

U.S. Air Force photo by Staff Sgt. Greg L. Davis

Photo by Tech. Sgt. Mark Moore, 138th Fighter Wing, Oklahoma Air National Guard

Above: Master Sgt. Patrick Owens looks across the runway of the 138th Fighter Wing, Oklahoma Air National Guard, while conducting countersniper operations. Owens is a member of the 138th Security Police Squadron participating in Operation Noble Eagle.

Right: Traditional Guardsmen, Senior Airman Darrell Webb and Staff Sgt. Denise Office of the 151st Services Flight, Utah Air National Guard, prepare "midnight chow" for personnel activated in support of Operation Noble Eagle, Oct. 3, 2001.

information fast enough."

"This phone bridge brought the command structure throughout the United States into one telephone call," he says.

With all eyes focused on the dense Northeast corridor, the open line has enabled NEADS controllers to assist the FAA numerous times since Sept. 11. "We had a Boston departure turning toward JFK (International Airport, N.Y.,) and there was a horse in the cargo hold that was kicking and making a rather large disturbance," Ayers says. "The crew thought it was an unruly passenger."

On an international flight bound for Boston, a Russian passenger retrieved something from the overhead bin and got into a scuffle with a flight attendant. By the time word reached NEADS, controllers believed somebody was rushing the cockpit, Ayers says.

"Before Sept. 11, there were limited communications between the air defense sectors and FAA centers," says Steve Culbertson, FAA air defense liaison officer for NEADS. "We had no way to talk. Now, we are hooked up to all the FAA centers and the FAA Command Center in Herndon, Virginia."

Adds assistant airspace manager Master Sgt. Jerry Lee, a civilian activated on Sept. 11: "We are able to talk to the FAA in their language and relay that information to our command and control specialists in their language."

Their finest hour

Displays of volunteerism and patriotism were apparent not only across NORAD, but service-wide. "Sept. 11, 2001, was a horrible tragedy," Scott says. "But the great American story of Sept. 11, 2001, is that people were knocking down our air defense sector doors. Guard units everywhere wanted to help. We had every Air Force unit out there saying, 'What can I do?' "

More than 60,000 Guardsmen reported to their bases Sept. 11, says retired Air National Guard Brig. Gen. Paul S. Kimmel, former assistant for operational readiness to the director of the Air National Guard. "I think we did what Guardsmen always do," Kimmel says, "and that's respond and respond well when there's a need. ... The initiative people took on their own without direction was amazing and showed the real value of the Air National Guard.

"This was probably our finest hour since Bunker Hill, and that says a lot."

Guardsmen are tough and resilient, WADS Commander Cromwell says. "People were focused and because of the tragedies, the motivation was there. About 100 of our traditional Guardsmen at WADS were suddenly mobilized and pulled out of their civilian jobs without notice. Everyone, including their employers and families, made great sacrifices."

From the first days of the tragedy well into Noble Eagle, the Air National Guard has been deeply en-

Utah Air National Guard photo by Master Sgt. Mark Savage

trenched in the operation, but "the commitment is to the Air Force," Arnold says. The Air National Guard provides the majority of CAPs and fulfills most of the alert requirements because of the high number of its units in nearly every state, Arnold says.

That's not to say the regular Air Force hasn't done its share. The 1st Fighter Wing, Langley Air Force Base, Va., for instance, provided F-15 Combat Air Patrol coverage over Washington, D.C., on Sept. 11, and continues to provide its resources. The 33rd Fighter Wing, Eglin Air Force Base, Fla., deployed some of its F-15s to Langley to help in the CAP efforts. [31]

The 366th Wing, Mountain Home Air Force Base, Idaho, has employed three of its squadrons for Operation Noble Eagle: the 390th Fighter Squadron, the 22nd Air Refueling Squadron and the 726th Air Control Squadron.

"We're a combat unit," says Lt. Col. Kathy Stoddard, 726th Air Control Squadron commander. "We usually deploy into a battle theater and our team provides radar coverage of enemy territory. Guarding America through Operation Noble Eagle is something we never expected we would have to do."

"All U.S. military operations require control of air, space and information," she continues. "We find, fix, assess, track, target, and engage everything of military significance. Our contribution to aerospace power is vital to our forces' effectiveness and our ability to fight and win with minimum loss of life — and that's anywhere in the world, including over the skies of the United States."

The 726th, known as "Hard Rock," was in-

volved in round-the-clock Noble Eagle operations for 170 days. [32] The unit maintained a 97-percent mission readiness rating after deploying members to other air control squadrons in Washington, New York and Nevada. [33] Hard Rock was released from its Noble Eagle tasking on Feb. 28, 2002.

The blood flows backward

The cooperative Noble Eagle spirit was coming from near and far. In October 2001, upon the United States' request, history was made when NATO deployed five of its E-3A AWACS aircraft to support America's homeland defense mission. [34] Nearly 200 troops from Geilenkirchen, Germany, landed at Tinker Air Force Base, Okla., to assist

Air Force photo by Staff Sgt. Greg L. Davis

the 552nd Air Control Wing with its new tasking. The deployment represents the first time NATO invoked Article 5 of its charter, which states a foreign attack on one member is an attack on all. [35]

"Right now, we are engaged in four theaters of operation," Brig. Gen. Ben Robinson, 552nd Air Control Wing commander at the time, said in November 2001. "Having NATO here ... reduced the risk and reduced the cost of our training." [36]

America welcomed the troops with open arms, says Col. Jim McNaughton, NATO detachment commander: "It is no longer we, they or a NATO force. We are one group here. ... We've taken these planes to a lot of places, but the reception here has been incredible." [37]

The NATO aircrews flew more than 360 sorties and logged more than 4,300 flying hours. After more than seven months in the States, they finally got to go home. [38]

"We are truly honored ... by the appreciation we have been given," says German Maj. Gen. Johann G. Dora, commander of the NATO Airborne Early Warning and Control Force Command. "From a NATO perspective, this 'Operation Eagle Assist' has had a truly historic dimension. After more than 50 years of one-way traffic across the Atlantic, in military support terms, the European NATO member nations were able to return some of the overwhelming support provided by the United States ... to Europe after World War II." [39]

Above: An F-16 from the 79th Fighter Squadron, 20th Fighter Wing, Shaw Air Force Base, S.C., flies a Combat Air Patrol mission in support of Operation Noble Eagle.

Left: Secretary of the Air Force Dr. James G. Roche thanks NATO crews for their support of Operation Noble Eagle during his visit to Tinker Air Force Base, Okla., Feb. 22, 2002.

Photo courtesy of 552nd Air Control Wing

Photo by Sgt. 1st Class Eric Wedeking, National Guard Bureau

District of Columbia Air National Guard Maj. Billy Hutchison folds the American flag that he carried with him while flying in the 113th Wing formation over the Pentagon during a Sept. 11 memorial service one year after the attack. Hutchison had flown his F-16 over the Pentagon Sept. 11, 2001.

Eagle still soars

The NATO AWACS had gone home. The constant CAPs were slowing down. Pilots were flying tactical training maneuvers again. But the Noble Eagle was still soaring after logging 22,000 sorties over the United States and Canada between Sept. 11, 2001, and June 28, 2002. [40] And it may be soaring for awhile.

By early 2003, the Air Force had authorized the extension of more than 14,000 Air National Guard and Air Force Reserve members into a second year, as needed, because of continuing operations Noble Eagle and Enduring Freedom requirements. Of those authorizations, 9,292 were from the Air National Guard. [41]

The total Air Force — active, Guard and Reserve — continues to assist federal agencies as needed in protecting the skies of America. "Adjustments in the NORAD air defense posture are driven by the potential threats to North American airspace," explains Maj. Don Arias, 1st Air Force and CONR spokesman. "The threat assessment takes into account the overall security posture, including the many improvements in airspace security — in the air and on the ground — made since Sept. 11. The best air defense begins on the ground through the efforts of numerous local, state and federal agencies. NORAD and its continental region is integrated with — and will remain available to — civil authorities as a force of last resort."

If the FAA calls, NORAD and its forces will be there and have responded to hundreds of domestic air security events since Sept. 11. The command still maintains its historic look outward, guarding America's borders from unknown threats.

Arnold says America expects nothing less. "The public always assumed we could protect this country, and we have," he says. "The continued vigil over our homeland's skies is still saving lives and sending a clear message to those who would inflict harm on our citizenry: 'Never again.' "

1 Bill Kaczor, "Air-Attack Fears Keep General Awake at Night: Officer Believes a Sudden Assault is Bound to Happen," *Miami Herald*, 31 January 2000, n.p.

2 William A. Scott, 2001. *Operation Noble Eagle: September 11, 2001, Air War Over America*. Panama City, Fla.: Microsoft PowerPoint presentation.

3 Ibid.

4 Ann Scott Tyson, "A New Diligence in the American Blue Yonder," *The Christian Science Monitor*, 16 April 2002, online edition, n.p.

5 NORAD Public Affairs Office, Operation Noble Eagle public affairs statements, n.p.

6 Sue Cathcart, "Home Air Defense: Guard Air Sovereignty Mission Turned Inside Out Sept. 11 After Terrorists Turn Jetliners Into Missiles," *National Guard* magazine, December 2001, 19; NORAD Public Affairs Office, public affairs statements, n.p.

7 William B. Scott, "NORAD and FAA Sharpen View Inside Borders," *Aviation Week & Space Technology*, June 10, 2002, 50.

8 NORAD Public Affairs Office, public affairs statements, n.p.

9 Ibid., n.p.

10 Mary Lou Vocale, "Guard Tempo of Operation Noble Eagle," *Code One, Lockheed Martin Aeronautics Company*, Fourth Quarter 2002, 11.

11 NORAD Public Affairs Office, public affairs statements, n.p.

12 Emily Bittner, "Pilot 'Hijack' Error Scrambles 2 F-16s to Chandler Skies," *Arizona Republic*, July 26, 2002, p. B1.

13 John Cromwell, interview with author, 16 October 2002.

14 NORAD Public Affairs Office, public affairs statements, n.p.

15 Vocale, "Guard Tempo of Operation Noble Eagle," 18.

16 Rod Grunwald, Noble Eagle-activated historian, compilation of units under 1st Air Force and CONR command and control after 11 September 2001.

17 Ibid.; NORAD Public Affairs Office, public affairs statements, n.p.

18 John Goheen, "America Attacked: Answering the Call," *National Guard* magazine, October 2001, 23.

19 Tom Froling, telephone interview with author, 8 October 2002.

20 Eric Hehs, "Major General Larry Arnold, Commander, 1st Air Force, Tyndall Air Force Base,

Florida," *Code One, Lockheed Martin Aeronautics Company*, First Quarter 2002, 8.

21 Elena O'Bryan, "New Aircraft Shelters at Buckley Take Bite Out of Winter," *Skywatch*, October-November 2002, p. 4.

22 Ibid., p. 4.

23 Phyllis Phipps-Barnes, "113th Wing Flies CAP; Now Stands Alert," *Capital Guardian*, Spring 2002, p. 16.

24 Scott, "NORAD and FAA Sharpen View Inside Borders," 50.

25 Ibid., 50.

26 Air Force Command, Control, Intelligence, Surveillance and Reconnaissance Center and Electronic Systems Center Public Affairs Office, "New Command and Control System Enables NORAD to Look In," n.d., n.p.

27 Scott, "NORAD and FAA Sharpen View Inside Borders," 50.

28 AFC2ISRC and ESC Public Affairs Office, "New Command and Control System Enables NORAD to Look In," n.d., n.p.

29 Ibid., n.p.

30 Donald Rumsfeld, "Report of the Quadrennial Defense Review" (Washington, D.C., Department of Defense, 2001), Section 18.

31 Larry K. Arnold, telephone interview with author, 11 September 2002.

32 Javier Esparza, *"'Hard Rock' Stands Down from Noble Eagle,"* Air Combat Command News Service, March 18, 2002, n.p.

33 Ibid., n.p.

34 Steven Rolenc, "History is Made: Tinker, NATO Defend America Hand in Hand," *Eyes of the Eagle*, November 2001, p. 3.

35 Ibid., p. 3.

36 Ibid., p. 3.

37 Ibid., p. 4.

38 Darren D. Heusel, *"Tinker Bids Farewell to NATO Crews,"* Oklahoma Air Logistics Center Public Affairs release, May 17, 2002, n.p.

39 Ibid., n.p.

40 NORAD Public Affairs Office, public affairs statements, n.p.

41 Ibid, n.p.

42 More information about the Sept. 11 commemorative artwork is available online at rickherter.com.

As part of its official art program, the Air Force selected artist Rick Herter to paint the arrival of the first fighters in New York and Washington Sept. 11, 2001. "Ground Zero, Eagles on Station," above, depicts the first Combat Air Patrol over Manhattan flown by F-15 pilot and Massachusetts Air National Guardsman Lt. Col. Tim Duffy of the 102nd Fighter Wing. "First Pass, Defenders over Washington," right, depicts the F-16 first flown over the Pentagon Sept. 11 by North Dakota Air National Guardsman Maj. Dean Eckmann of the 119th Fighter Wing. The paintings were unveiled Sept. 4, 2002, at the Pentagon. [42]

Artwork courtesy of Rick Herter

THE NOBLE EAGLE FLIES

CHAPTER 5

AMERICAN STORIES:
Sept. 11 brings new resolve

Air defenders steadfast amid terror and tragedy

Five months after America was attacked, armed fighter jets flew through frigid Utah skies to protect the 2002 Winter Olympic Games. By Sept. 11, 2002, live anti-aircraft missile batteries were deployed in the nation's capital. America's air defense mission had changed so much since that day and the change continues. These seven stories provide a glimpse into the mission on Sept. 11 and evolving operations beyond.

☐☐☐

Family hoped against hope

Like bad news often does, it began with a phone call. This one was about a hijacking.

It was early in the morning Sept. 11, 2001, and the phone was ringing at the 1st Air Force public affairs office. Maj. Don Arias was preparing for the day when he took the call from the Northeast Air Defense Sector. There had been a hijacking on a flight out of Boston: American Airlines Flight 77 was presumably headed for John F. Kennedy International Airport, N.Y., and the sector might scramble some fighters. It was an odd coincidence:

across the North American Aerospace Defense Command, everyone was preparing for an air defense exercise simulating an attack on the United States. But this hijacking was no exercise — it was "real-world."

Arias, the 1st Air Force and Continental United States NORAD Region public affairs officer, hung up the phone, grabbed his press kit and began working on a statement. He'd have to get something together before heading over to the CONR Air Operations Center at Tyndall Air Force Base, Fla., where Commander Maj. Gen. Larry K. Arnold and his battle staff were entering an operational war mode.

"Maybe 15 minutes elapsed and I look up and see the tower smoking on CNN," Arias says. "I had no confirmation, but knew that hijacked plane had hit the tower. That's when I called my brother."

☐☐☐

Adam P. Arias, a 37-year-old vice president for the trading company Eurobrokers, had been scheduled to attend a meeting uptown that morning. But he'd returned from Jamaica only three days earlier and was just too busy, sending an assistant instead. Now on the phone with his wife, the caller ID screen was displaying his older brother's number. Adam

YOUR GUARDIANS OF FREEDOM

AIR NATIONAL GUARD

"WE WILL NOT WAVER. WE WILL NOT TIRE. WE WILL NOT FALTER. WE WILL NOT FAIL."
President George W. Bush

WWW.YOURGUARDIANSOFFREEDOM.COM

Artwork by Senior Airman Philip Speck, Kentucky Air National Guard

told Margit he loved her; Margit told Adam to come home. They'd just celebrated their three-year anniversary. They said their goodbyes.

Adam clicked over to his big brother. "Hey everybody, it's the Air Force!" Adam exclaimed to his colleagues in their 84th floor office in the World Trade Center's south tower. "He told me, 'You won't believe what I'm looking at,'" Arias says. "It was some horrendous stuff. He was watching the other tower burn and saw people falling through the air. He saw people jumping. I could hear a lot of commotion in the background and apparently everybody was at the window looking."

"I told him, 'Hey, we got this call, this could be the hijacked plane,'" Arias says. "He said to me, 'This is prime time. If this is an attack, they're doing it at the right time.'

"I told him to go home and that's the last words I said to him. I don't even know if he heard me because it was such a quick conversation."

Arias later heard what Adam did next. "He went around and told people that he'd talked to me and knew it was a hijacking, because people were content to sit there at their desks," Arias says. "I met a young woman a year later and she told me that Adam physically picked her up around her waist and threw her out of her office. She had wanted to stay because she had so much to do.

"More than a few people credit Adam with saving their lives by throwing them out of the office that day."

A fire engine is parked amid the crime scene at Ground Zero, Sept. 16, 2001. A lone firefighter can be seen in the distance.

As the horrific events continued to transpire in the northeast, Arias and his staff in Florida were on the phone with NORAD, trying to get statements out to the media. Struggling to maintain his professional composure, Arias was on a roller coaster ride of uncertainty. *Where was his brother?* He kept trying Adam's cell phone, leaving message upon message on his voice mailbox, but had to settle for only bits and pieces of information. "My whole family was on the phone and in the meantime, I'm trying to do my job here and popping off calls to my parents, sisters and brothers," Arias says. "One person said they saw Adam transferring elevators on about the 40th floor.

U.S. Navy photo by Chief Photographer's Mate Eric J. Tilford

gotten out in time? He was picturing the scene in his mind. A proud New York City firefighter for seven years, Arias still wears a miniature of the gold Maltese cross badge of the FDNY around his neck — number 2105. The cross is a popular and time-honored symbol of the fire service, and represents St. Florian, the protector of firefighters. Now many of them were gone.

□□□

The day turned to night, and around 8 o'clock, Arias drove home, fearing the worst for Adam, the baby of six children. Mentally, physically and emotionally drained, he sat on the couch with his wife, Karen, also a New Yorker. They couldn't take their eyes off the news.

"I knew that night when I got home and Adam hadn't come home from work, that he was gone," Arias says. "Despite reports that people saw him, we knew. But we were all hoping against hope."

Rumors that emergency rooms were flooded with victims were unfounded. "You were either dead or you got away," Arias says. "There were lots of rumors flying, but I knew in my heart, as only a brother would know, that if he didn't make it home that night and didn't let anyone know where he was, that he couldn't."

Adam's family and friends were canvassing Manhattan, posting fliers and visiting every hospital in town. Arias and Karen, feeling helpless in Florida, stayed up late into the night, crying and watching news reports of people walking home over the familiar Brooklyn and Verrazano bridges, praying one of them was Adam.

Little did they know, Adam's remains were recovered hours earlier but not identified — a sad fact they'd learn days later. Adam P. Arias was the eighth person recovered at Ground Zero. Through peoples' stories and because his body was found near the base of the tower, the Arias family believes he got out alive and was helping firefighters in their rescue attempts.

Other people said they saw him in the street helping the firemen.

"I had a lump in my throat that whole day."

Finally, some good news: A message from their sister Lauren that Adam was spotted — alive. *"Your brother is OK. Your sister called and talked to someone who saw your brother boarding the ferry."*

"We were totally relieved and I called my brother Tom, who was on his way to Manhattan to go look for Adam and Tom said, 'You know what? I'll believe he's OK when I talk to him,'" Arias says. "Tom knew it was ugly."

Arias, who grew up on Staten Island in the house where his parents still live, knows the city like only a native would. *Where was Adam?* Could he have

"I'm not sure what he was doing or feeling or thinking, but I know his last minutes on earth were fulfilling his last act of Christian charity," Arias says. "The very last thing Adam was doing was helping other people. We should all go out that way. He is a true American hero."

❑❑❑

On Sept. 13, Arias boarded a military flight to Pennsylvania, where an aunt picked him up and drove him to New York. He spent the day with his family, watching his broken parents cry like never before. The next day, Arias went to his former firehouse, Ladder 36, in the Inwood section of Manhattan, where two old friends just lost their own brothers, among the 343 firefighters killed.

"You got there and you could hear a pin drop," Arias says. "It was very quiet. Usually firehouses are loud, busy places, but this time they were just busy. There were a lot of people working. Even guys who had been retired for years were back to help."

Arias went to the firehouse for a reason — to somehow get closer to Adam, his fun-loving, witty brother, a talented singer who loved singing Frank Sinatra and Tony Bennett classics.

"I went to Ladder 36 to get down to Ground Zero," Arias says. "The truck officer got on the phone and called the police and we got back in the car and got right down to the command center. I hooked up with the New York National Guard once I got there and eventually got on a Humvee right to Ground Zero."

"We had to wear hard hats and breathing apparatus and you could just feel the grit in your teeth. I wanted to see if I could look around and was hoping against hope that I'd maybe find something out about my brother. But it was so immense it would be like looking for a needle in a haystack. People looked like little ants on this huge hill.

Photos courtesy of the Arias family

Top: Adam P. Arias on his wedding day. He and Margit had just celebrated their three-year anniversary when he was killed Sept. 11, 2001.

Above: Adam, left, at his wedding with brother Maj. Don Arias, will be remembered for his great sense of humor.

"Two 110-story buildings had telescoped down to seven stories of twisted steel and concrete. There was not one piece of office furniture, not one personal item you'd see in an office, that had survived. It was just huge pieces of steel, girders, concrete, and paper."

Amid the six-acre war zone were American flags, stacks of pizza pies and cases of bottled water from all the New Yorkers who came to the rescue workers' aid.

Arias stayed home with his family for three weeks. It was a tough time. "Staten Island, my home borough, has more cops and firemen than any other borough in New York," he says.

"We took an extraordinary hit there. It was a depressing place to be. There were funerals and memorial services every single day. It was unbelievable."

> **"The very last thing Adam was doing was helping other people."**
> **— Maj. Don Arias, brother**

□□□

On Sept. 19, detectives knocked on Margit's door with the official news; Adam's funeral was Sept. 21 followed by his cremation. The family honored Adam a second time at a memorial service Oct. 13 in Panama City, Fla., where Arias is stationed at Tyndall Air Force Base.

Suddenly Arias found his professional and personal worlds colliding.

"There's probably no place I'd rather be working right now than in continental air defense," Arias says. "The first mushroom cloud of World War III will be in New York unless we stop that from happening."

"I'm a real stakeholder in this mission. I always was, but more so now than ever. It is quite personal for me."

Indeed, Adam's death certificate reads: *"Cause of Death: Homicide."*

In the months that followed the attacks, the Arias family found a special way to honor Adam's memory. His little brother was a "self-starter," Arias says, who worked his way up the corporate ladder without a college degree. Adam and Margit didn't have children. They loved their nieces and nephews and had a special place in their heart for Vincent, Arias' son, who is autistic. "Margit knew Adam was very concerned with Vincent and his situation," Arias says. "We'd had a lot of conversations about Vincent, and Margit thought a fitting way to honor Adam was through a scholarship."

The family founded the Adam P. Arias Applied Behavior Analysis Scholarship for Autism at Florida State University, Panama City campus. The endowed scholarship is awarded to students based on community service, scholastic achievement and financial need.

The Arias family continued to grieve. One year after the attacks, they attended the Sept. 11 memorial service at Ground Zero that honored the approximately 2,800 people killed there. A bell was rung as each victim's name was read. Margit was one of the readers.

"They started reading the names at the precise minute of the first impact," Arias says. "As they rang that bell, the wind just started to whip up. It was a huge wind. The southern tip of lower Manhattan is known for being breezy, but this was extraordinary and it seemed like it was changing direction. It wasn't just blowing in off the water, it was going up, down and in. It was as if the forces of nature were converging on this one spot to make a statement."

With the graceful music of cellist Yo-Yo Ma filling the blustery air, the winds continued and the names were read, one by one. Including Adam's.

Sector was 'fighting blind' Sept. 11

Amid missing airliners, bomb threats and a shockingly horrific terrorist attack, radar specialists at the Western Air Defense Sector, McChord Air Force Base, Wash., were "fighting blind" Sept. 11, 2001.

"There was no way we could see the interior of the United States on Sept. 11, 2001," says Maj. Sue Cheney, mission crew commander that day. "That would have required a whole new computer system. ... You know there's a threat coming in, but you can't see it. You're trying to get assets in places you can't see and if you had to scramble them, you'd never be able to talk to those fighters. You'd have to work through the Federal Aviation Administration to get any kind of message to them."

The WADS is responsible for protecting 1.9 million square miles of airspace, from Texas to the West Coast across to North Dakota, but the Q-93 — the huge computer installed in the 1980s with 1970s technology — could not display an interior air picture. With 63 percent of the continental airspace, the radar and radio links at WADS were weaker than those at air defense sectors in New York and Florida. Essentially, the radar scopes at the sector were showing flights inbound from overseas on Sept. 11 and very little over the vast western skies of the interior United States.

"The whole idea of an aircraft being hijacked in the middle of the United States and flown into a big target ... that was one we never really exercised," Cheney says. "It was one we were not really capable of dealing with. If you look at our old Q-93 scope, you've got this enormous hole in the interior of the country. ... We were fighting blind."

As WADS commander Col. John Cromwell

prepared to possibly scramble nearly every fighter west of the Mississippi, communications with the FAA were suddenly more important than ever. "We were told to put Combat Air Patrols up over numerous cities and metropolitan areas and key infrastructure in the western United States," Cromwell says. "Our plate was full in the West and when the FAA asked for assistance, the fighters would talk to FAA controllers. We had no pictures and no radio. The FAA also did a great job in pointing out where situations were. Between the FAA and the flexibility of the pilots, our intercepts were successful."

In the days before Sept. 11, four fighter jets were on alert out West, ready to respond to unknowns approaching the borders. The F-15s and F-16s are from the 142nd Fighter Wing, Oregon Air National Guard, Portland; and the 144th Fighter Wing, California Air National Guard, Fresno, with an alert station at March Air Reserve Base in Riverside, Calif. But four jets would not be enough that tragic day. In only a few hours, the skies were

Washington Air National Guard photos by Tech. Sgt. Randy LaBrune

teeming with fighters and by the afternoon, more than 100 fighter jets were on alert, Cromwell says.

With initiative from civilian FAA air defense liaison Ed Enkerud, the sector tapped into FAA centers across the West as it guided fighter pilots to targets. Enkerud says an FAA "domestic event network" launched two hours after the initial attack was invaluable. "I got a call from my boss in Washington, D.C., and we all started dialing into one number and started instantaneous communication that is still ongoing," Enkerud says. "Now we don't have to dial different facilities. We can talk right now and the line is always open."

Cromwell says he's proud of the sector's response Sept. 11: "People used their training in a brand new scenario. They were innovative, creative and under control."

Above: Canadian Forces Warrant Officer Scott Budgell and Maj. Cecilia Nackowski monitor the radar scopes at the Western Air Defense Sector.

Left: Staff Sgt. Jill Lathrop on the job in the dim and windowless sector operations center.

A calm surrealism Sept. 11 at SEADS

Absolutely "unbelievable." That's how Lt. Col. Clark "Buck" Rogers describes Sept. 11, 2001.

The director of operations at the Southeast Air Defense Sector, Tyndall Air Force Base, Fla., says it all happened very fast. "I remember, vividly, turning to our commander (Col. Larry Kemp) and saying: 'This is a coordinated attack. And it may not stop in the Northeast. We need to get our airplanes up because we don't know what's coming next.'

"And that's exactly what we did."

The sector put pilots from its three area air defense alert facilities on battle stations — in the cockpit ready to start at a moment's notice. At Ellington Field, Texas; Homestead Air Reserve Base, Fla.; and Tyndall Air Force Base; fliers were suiting up and waiting for the Klaxon alarm to sound. The shrill tone would echo in Texas, as pilots were scrambled to escort Air Force One.

Help was coming from across the Southeast. "Fighter wings from across the Air Force —both active duty and Air National Guard — called to assist," Rogers says. "We told them the country was under attack and the best they could do was load ammo on live airplanes. And that's what they did. We asked units that already had airplanes on alert to bring up additional airplanes, bring up the spares and get four airplanes loaded and four guys in crew rest.

"There wasn't a base out there that wasn't on alert."

They had to get in the minds of the terrorists. What would they hit? The SEADS area of responsibility includes Atlanta, Dallas, Miami, nuclear sites, and military bases. "We immediately said, 'Our responsibility is not to protect New York City, but to protect the Southeast. What should we be concentrating on?' " Rogers says.

Rogers was scrambling fighters as the skies of America were being cleared of all civilian traffic. "All flights had to be approved by the appropriate air defense sector, even if it was a military flight," Rogers says. "We disapproved almost everything, but Life Flights got permission to fly."

Extra measures were taken to ensure the flights were legitimate. "We had to call a hospital and ask if they were really expecting a plane with a sick child from Mexico," Rogers says. "Just because it was painted like Life Flight doesn't mean it was Life Flight. Just because it was painted like American Airlines, doesn't mean it was."

Kemp was responsible for final approval of Southeast-area flights in the immediate post-attack and even approved flights of the Federal Reserve to help get the economy moving again.

The commander says the day's events were surreal. But there was method to what should have been madness. "It was very methodical and structured," Kemp explains. "The training and proficiency kicked in. Everybody had a clear picture of what the big picture was and what they had to accomplish."

Rogers has one positive memory of the day: "I walked out of here at maybe 9:30 or 10 that night. I was pretty dismayed and could not believe what had happened. It was like the end of innocence. But the first thing I saw as I drove out the gate was all the houses on the base with American flags. There were flags in every neighborhood, on businesses, on car dealerships ... everything said 'God Bless America,' 'We Love Our Country,' and 'United We Stand.' It was an amazing outpouring of support."

Left: The Southeast Air Defense Sector area of responsibility includes the Gulf Coast, where F-16 fighter jets of the Texas Air National Guard fly Combat Air Patrol missions in support of Operation Noble Eagle.

Below: In a late 2001 visit to SEADS, Air National Guard Command Chief Master Sgt. Valerie D. Benton, top adviser for enlisted affairs, receives an update on the Straits of Florida from Tech. Sgt. Gerry Myers, a SEADS air surveillance technician.

Photo by Master Sgt. Roger Tibbetts, 1st Air Force Public Affairs Office

An overall view of the Northeast Air Defense Sector operations center, a cool, dimly lighted room with no windows.

Photos by Scott A. Gw

A NEADS technician peers into a colorful map of the regional air picture. The imagery is part of a computer software program NORAD installed after Sept. 11, 2001, that gives controllers the capability to view more than 15,000 tracks at any moment per air defense sector instead of the 300 tracks before Sept. 11.

Fear strikes NEADS Sept. 12;
'mole people' never rest

After Sept. 11, crews at the Northeast Air Defense Sector in Rome, N.Y., didn't think things could get much worse. Helping secure America's skies amid a horrifying terrorist attack, they'd worked late into the evening, got minimal sleep and were back at it the next morning. Certainly Sept. 12 would be calmer — the attacks were over and the North American Aerospace Defense Command was guarding the skies like never before.

But as Tech. Sgt. Ronald G. Belluscio, a senior weapons director technician, peered into his radar scope, he knew something was wrong. "There was a plane, flying low and slow, headed right toward this building," he says. "My first thought was, 'Who is this?' Then it clicked. 'This isn't normal. Who is this guy and why is he headed toward us?'"

Security forces members lined up on a hill with guns aimed at the sky, hoping they could down the plane if it came to that.

The Federal Aviation Administration had surrendered America's airspace to NORAD, all civilian aviation was grounded and the skies were free of anything other than military or emergency aircraft. But the unidentified airplane, headed toward Rome from the south-southeast, kept on coming.

"We thought anyone in the air was either a terrorist or a criminal and this aircraft was beelining straight at us," says Col. Bob Marr, NEADS commander. "We had some F-16s that had been flying Combat Air Patrol over New York City and were headed back to Burlington, (Vt.). We vectored them toward the plane."

Master Sgt. Joe McCain, mission crew commander technician, says Marr was very direct:

"He told the weapons section to get a hold of those aircraft to see if they had enough fuel to get to Rome. He said, 'I want those birds here and now. Light afterburner if you have to!'"

With the Vermont Air National Guard jets diverted their way, Marr ordered the evacuation of the building, leaving himself and a small crew in the operations center. "If we were attacked, the others would be able to come in and finish the mission," Marr says.

Meanwhile, Senior Master Sgt. Thomas Hayes, chief of NEADS Security Forces, directed his staff to hide the evacuees in the trees surrounding the building. From outside, Hayes stayed in radio contact with security forces member Staff Sgt. Mike Bates, the desk sergeant inside the building. Bates relayed the airplane's position to Hayes as security forces members lined up on a hill with guns aimed at the sky, hoping they could down the plane if it came to that.

Bates, a Syracuse, N.Y., police officer in his civilian life, admits he was scared. "It was nerve-wracking," he says. "I'm not going to lie. I was nervous and thinking about my family. It still wasn't reality that Sept. 11 had happened. We thought we were under attack and when Col. Marr yelled for people to get out of the building, you could feel the sense of urgency. We knew airplanes weren't supposed to be in the air, yet this guy was coming at us and I was waiting inside the building expecting to hear the guns start firing."

Inside the operations center, Marr says people were shaking at the scopes as they watched on

Above: Two F-16s sit armed and ready outside their new alert shelters at Selfridge Air National Guard Base, Mich. Air controllers at the Northeast Air Defense Sector, Rome, N.Y., have found themselves working with units like Michigan's 127th Wing more than ever since Sept. 11, 2001.

Right: Col. Bob Marr, commander of NEADS, evacuated the sector operations center on Sept. 12, 2001, when an unidentified airplane was heading straight for the building.

radar as the plane got closer and closer. McCain says he was more afraid on Sept. 12 than he was Sept. 11. "The 11th was horrible," he says. "But we had to do our jobs. The 12th was personal."

Adds Belluscio: "It was like slow motion. You could see the distance between the target and the fighters and we didn't think the fighters would make it. I was on the edge of my seat, rocking back and forth thinking it would make the fighters go faster."

But suddenly, the calmer day came when the airplane changed course only miles from the sector operations center. The F-16s were in close pursuit and forced the plane to land at nearby Hinckley Reservoir, Marr says.

From here, the story of that unknown plane becomes NEADS legend. "The word is, the police cut the wings off the plane and put it on a flatbed truck," says Belluscio.

Marr says he never found out who the culprit was, but heard he was a local pilot with a seaplane. Whoever he was, he was flying against all federal regulations in the early days after Sept. 11.

□□□

For months, the crews at NEADS worked 12-hour days, six days on, three days off. Days like Sept. 12 were especially difficult, says sector chaplain Maj. Timothy Bejian.

"The stress was enormous," Bejian says. "After Sept. 11, that's what it was like for days on end. As the days went by, I was watching the folks and seeing how they were dealing with the stress.

"People would go out at night and watch the flying squirrels jump from tree to tree. We called them the 'mole people.' It was September and people would arrive in the dark and leave in the dark and didn't see their families. As chaplain, you have to try to bring people back to a point where they can cope. The problem wasn't going to go away and some had a very difficult time."

Bejian puts things into perspective with "The Mole People and the Flying Squirrels," a story he wrote for those guarding the Northeastern skies.

Photo by Scott A. Gwilt, Daily Sentinel, Rome, N.Y.

'The Mole People and the Flying Squirrels'

"... If it weren't for the 'mole people,' the regular people of the world wouldn't be able to walk outside their homes in safety. The world is full of monsters and beasts and all kinds of nasty creatures that would freeze their blood and hurt their children. But the mole people are always watching. They watch by day while the regular people work and their children play. They watch at night while the regular people sleep in their cozy beds or read fairy tales to their children. Why, you ask, are these watchers called the mole people? Well, the answer is quite simple. They gather together in groups, in windowless places, usually arriving while it's dark and staying long hours only to leave while it's dark. Many times they can't tuck their own children into bed and read them fairy tales because they are watching. This bothers the mole people, but they know that it needs to be done. And if ever they see something or someone bad who wants to hurt the regular people, they send a message to their friends the Eagles who outrace the wind to pursue and drive off the beasts and monsters."

— Maj. Timothy Bejian,
NEADS chaplain

Air refuelers fly in face of terror

Only weeks after flying Combat Air Patrols over Washington, D.C., on Sept. 11, 2001, F-16 pilot Maj. Dan Caine was soaring high above the rugged terrain of Afghanistan.

It was the early days of Operation Enduring Freedom and an early winter evening when Caine, a member of the 113th Wing, District of Columbia Air National Guard, heard familiar voices over his radio frequency. Turns out the same crew pumping 6,000 pounds of JP-8 into his F-16 was the very crew that refueled his fighter low over Washington, D.C., the day terrorists attacked America. It's a small Air Force, Caine reasons, and an even smaller Air National Guard.

America's refueling tanker crews are crucial to the fight against terrorism. From the 117th Air Refueling Wing in Birmingham, Ala., to the 161st Air Refueling Wing in Phoenix, Ariz., the tanker crews keep America's fighters airborne.

Scores of wings across the country have come under 1st Air Force and Continental United States North American Aerospace Defense Command Region command and control at various points since Sept. 11 — all in support of Operation Noble Eagle. The 101st Air Refueling Wing, Maine Air National Guard, is one. The "MAINEiacs" are proud to have refueled fighters over Manhattan the morning of Sept. 11. That day is a vivid memory for KC-135E boom operator Senior Master Sgt. Robert Phair, a 20-year Maine Air National Guard veteran.

"We were out on a local training mission when all hell broke loose," Phair recalls. "We heard through the Federal Aviation Administration Boston Center that an aircraft had impacted one of the towers and we were completely amazed that something so horrific could happen."

Like many that morning, the crew assumed the crash was accidental. "When we heard that a second plane had hit, we could detect in the voices of the controllers that it was more than coincidence. We got passed off to New York Center and the controllers' voices were elevated. They were very concerned and asked us to provide emergency air refueling coverage for fighters and we said, 'Absolutely.'"

The civilian FAA controllers requested the tanker's presence about 10 miles off New York City's coastline, Phair says. "We said, 'We can do better than that, we can fly right over Manhattan.'

"They said, 'You guys are cleared Manhattan right now.'"

Back on the ground at Bangor International Airport, the MAINEiacs' home base, the scene was one of "mass controlled confusion," says Tech. Sgt. Philip Henderson, a KC-135E crew chief. Watching TV one moment in the break room, crews suddenly found themselves on the ramp preflighting and gassing up the tankers. Soon they'd find themselves airborne, witness to terror below.

"As we approached Long Island Sound, I could see Ground Zero and the smoke drifting eastward," Henderson says. "I went into the boom operator's compartment and went to the window. We were looking out and everybody was pretty silent looking

Photos by Master Sgt. Don Taggart, 177th Fighter Wing, New Jersey Air National Guard

The 916th Air Refueling Wing, flying the KC-135R, supports a Combat Air Patrol mission over the Northeast United States on Oct. 7, 2001. The 916th, an Air Force Reserve unit, is based at Seymour Johnson Air Force Base, N.C.

Photo courtesy of 101st Air Refueling Wing, Maine Air National Guard

Above: A 101st Air Refueling Wing KC-135, Maine Air National Guard, provides in-flight refueling for a Canadian Forces F-18. The 101st regularly supports the Canadian Forces during Operation Noble Eagle Combat Air Patrol missions.

Right: Pilots from the 157th Air Refueling Wing, New Hampshire Air National Guard, fly their KC-135 during an Operation Noble Eagle mission over New York in November 2001.

at the smoke coming up but we couldn't get definite information on what was going on. It's burned into your memory, being up there and seeing the smoke from Ground Zero and seeing the live fighters coming up to you with missiles on them. It was unreal."

❏❏❏

At the end of the day, the 101st had diverted two of its airborne aircraft to support East Coast fighters and brought three other KC-135s to cockpit alert within minutes, launching them all.

"It normally takes two hours to generate a sortie up until takeoff," says Maj. Ian Gillis, 101st Air Refueling Wing chief of aircrew scheduling. "That day, we briefed in about 10 minutes and had aircraft ready to launch in just about an hour."

Not one year had passed since that terror-filled morning, and the wing had already flown more than 508 sorties in support of Operation Noble Eagle, for more than 2,800 hours of flying time. The Maine tankers had pumped more than 11.8 million pounds of fuel into nearly 1,500 fighter jets flying CAPs over the United States.

"At any one time, a third of military aircraft protecting the United States are tankers," Gillis explains. "When you see two fighters on a Noble Eagle CAP, there's always a tanker somewhere above them."

❏❏❏

According to Air Force statistics, across America, more than 15,000 airmen from the Air National Guard, Air Force Reserve and regular Air Force flew more than 26,400 fighter, tanker and airborne early warning sorties in the 13 months after the Sept. 11, 2001, attacks.

Photo by Tech. Sgt. Alan Beaulieu, 157th Air Refueling Wing, New Hampshire Air National Guard

Olympics protection golden example of interagency cooperation

As international athletes were gliding down the powdery slopes below, armed jet fighters were soaring above Utah keeping the skies of the 2002 Winter Olympics safe.

Only weeks after the Sept. 11 attacks, already tight security grew to include protection of Olympics airspace. As part of Joint Task Force-Olympics, soldiers and airmen supported federal, state and local agencies at the Hill Air Force Base, Utah, Air Security Operations Center. The ASOC, actually the corner of a hangar, brought civilian agencies

and military members together like never before, says Col. John E. Bonner, Western Air Defense Sector director of support. The sector, at McChord Air Force Base, Wash., is one of three continental air defense sectors in the North American Aerospace Defense Command and served as a lead air control agency for the Olympics.

"Before Sept. 11, a large national event was not a concern for NORAD," says Bonner, who led a WADS contingency to Utah that February. "Never before Sept. 11 did we see internal matters as

posing a threat. But the president declared the Olympics a 'National Special Security Event,' and we needed a significant presence to protect that airspace.

"The big story is the interagency cooperation and how everyone worked together to make it happen. The Secret Service was in charge of all security, both in the air and on the ground; U.S. Customs was the lead for air security; and the FBI was involved in ground security. The Army played a huge role and flew over 400 missions to support law enforcement and emergency services. ... Our piece was things in the air moving faster than helicopters."

Using an intricate network of radars, radios and sensors employed especially for the Olympics, NORAD, WADS and the Federal Aviation Administration could maintain constant contact and provide constant air coverage of the Games. "We grabbed data feeds from all the low-altitude and short-range radars and brought them back to WADS for display in the NORAD Contingency Suite, our newest computer system," says Chief Master Sgt. James Hunter, WADS support superintendent. "We needed redundancy in our radar data and high-resolution in our radar picture."

Hunter and 25 other WADS members worked especially closely with the FAA as it imposed temporary flight restrictions around Olympics airspace. The FAA authenticated 6,630 different flights entering restricted areas during the Olympics, Bonner says. There were more than 20 violators, but armed F-16s from Hill's 388th Fighter Wing, on alert and flying random Combat Air Patrol missions over Salt Lake, were ready to intercept when necessary. They were supported by more than 100 NORAD fighters on alert at 30 bases across the country.

The military and other agencies involved logged 3,300 flying hours in support of Olympics air protection, Bonner says. "Those hours were accident-free," Bonner adds, "in some pretty lousy flying weather."

Above: Western Air Defense Sector personnel Col. John E. Bonner and Maj. Roger Hurd, foreground, monitor command and control data at the Air Security Operations Center during the 2002 Winter Olympic Games in Salt Lake City.

Left: Four 388th Fighter Wing F-16s from Hill Air Force Base, Utah, fly over the Olympics.

Multilayered air defenses protect nation's capital

Heat-seeking "Stinger" missiles mounted on Humvees ... jet fighters on constant prowl over the city ... airborne warning and control platforms eyeing the skies up high as sensors scan for threats down low. It may sound like a combat zone in a distant land, but this multilayered air defense system has become a familiar sight right in the nation's capital.

Throughout Operation Noble Eagle, a theme has emerged from the North American Aerospace Defense Command: the best air defense starts on the ground. Nowhere has this been more apparent than Washington, D.C., where live anti-aircraft missile batteries have been deployed during high-profile events like the Sept. 11 anniversary and January 2003 State of the Union address.

The joint efforts have brought together hundreds of people from NORAD and throughout the armed services, the U.S. Customs Service, Federal Aviation Administration, and Secret Service. The air defense arsenal has included Air Force F-16s and Airborne Warning and Control System aircraft; ground-based Army "Sentinel" radars and "Avenger" missile batteries; and U.S. Customs Service UH-60A "Black Hawk" helicopters.

"We employ air defense artillery for high-value assets, people, infrastructure, and national government," says Maj. Gen. Craig R. McKinley, commander of 1st Air Force and the Continental United States NORAD Region and the Joint Air and Space Component Commander. "We provide a third layer of defense for targets that would possibly slip through the fighter Combat Air Patrols and the U.S. Customs and Secret Service barriers that are put in place.

"Air defense artillery is like a goalie in a hockey game. It is the last line of defense before a track of interest would actually make an impact with a building, and in the national capital region, everyone knows where those buildings are. That is why we heavily defend our nation's capital and seat of government."

The command and control architecture of that robust air defense artillery includes a mobile system called the "Joint Based Expeditionary Connectivity Center," the "center of the wheel for command and control," on such operations, McKinley says.

"The JBECC is the fusion hub where all the data is correlated and presented to me, the Joint Air and Space Component Commander, so I can present it to the decision-makers," he says. "It is extremely effective and we've had great success with it."

The JBECC was developed in the mid-1990s under the "Advanced Concept Technology Demonstration" program of the Office of Undersecretary of Defense, which explores opportunities to quickly get emerging technology into the hands of the warfighters. It was born as a "Cruise Missile Defense Initiative" and evolved into

> *"Air defense artillery is like a goalie in a hockey game. It is the last line of defense before a track of interest would actually make an impact with a building, and in the national capital region, everyone knows where those buildings are."*
>
> **— Maj. Gen. Craig R. McKinley, 1st Air Force commander**

Staff Sgt. Jarrett Jongema, Battery C, 4-5 ADA, 1st Cavalry Division, executes communications checks near the Pentagon during Operation Noble Eagle.

U.S. Army photo by Sgt. Erick Henson

the "Area Cruise Missile Defense."

The advanced programs branch of 1st Air Force began with a Humvee and added different types of radios and communications devices that would give NORAD the clear low-altitude air picture it had been missing.

"JBECC allows us to link into other sensors like Army Sentinel radars, Navy Aegis cruisers and Avenger missile systems," explains Lt. Col. Hutch Davis, 1st Air Force chief of operations integration for advanced programs. "It then correlates these radar inputs into one consolidated air picture."

The JBECC then sends the picture to one of three sector operations centers within CONR, allowing controllers to potentially deploy weapons against cruise missiles, Unmanned Aerial Vehicles and other low-altitude threats.

The concept went "real-world" after the terrorist attacks on Sept. 11, 2001, says Maj. John Ackermann, 1st Air Force chief of advanced programs demonstrations. On Sept. 12, a JBECC prototype being used by the Army was deployed to Naval Air Station Oceana, Va., and linked the CONR Air Operations Center into AWACS and other East Coast radars. "JBECC tied into the existing sensors that were there but not in the NORAD system," Ackermann explains. "NORAD now had an East Coast air picture it could utilize."

Since then, JBECC has been deployed in several operations, including airspace protection of the 2002 Winter Olympics Games. "The success of this experiment is a big step forward in the development of a single integrated air picture," Ackermann says. "The single picture will give all commanders a common view of the aerial battlefield."

CHAPTER 6

HOME THEATER: NORTHCOM guards air, land and sea

1st Air Force modernizing to defend skies of a new era

The world is a battleground. That post-Sept. 11 realization led to the most sweeping set of changes to U.S. military structure seen since 1946. [1]

Only eight months after the twin towers fell, Defense Secretary Donald Rumsfeld and Air Force Gen. Richard Myers, chairman of the Joint Chiefs of Staff, announced changes to the Unified Command Plan — the framework for military missions and geographic responsibilities for combatant commanders.

"The new commander will be responsible for land, aerospace and sea defense of the United States," Rumsfeld explained at the April 17, 2002, announcement. "He will command U.S. forces that operate within the United States in support of civil authorities." [2]

Northern Command, with Gen. Ralph E. Eberhart at the controls, was established Oct. 1, 2002, at Peterson Air Force Base, Colo. The NORTHCOM commander is responsible for homeland defense and still wears the blue Air Force uniform as commander of the North American Aerospace Defense Command, the organization charged with aerospace warning and control for the United States and Canada.

An F-16 assigned to the California Air National Guard 144th Fighter Wing flies a Combat Air Patrol over San Francisco in support of Operation Noble Eagle.

"Military forces will be used when and where needed to augment and assist first responders," Eberhart explains. "The goal is to be proactive, not just reactive. Nothing is more important for a government to do than provide safety and security and improve the quality of life for its citizens." [3]

"We are just like the other regional combatant commanders, with one important difference — the United States homeland is in our area of responsibility," the general says. [4]

The old days of continental air sovereignty — protecting America's air borders with jets on alert at a few strategic locations — are a distant memory.

The reorganization shifts the U.S. Joint Forces Command geographic area of responsibility to NORTHCOM and U.S. European Command, enabling U.S. Joint Forces Command to focus on transforming U.S. military forces — another post-Sept. 11 theme of changing the way the military does business. [5]

The NORTHCOM area of operations is vast, and includes the United States, Canada, Mexico, parts of the Caribbean, and the contiguous waters in the Atlantic and Pacific oceans. [6]

The creation of NORTHCOM is historic, says Maj. Gen. Craig R. McKinley, commander of 1st Air Force and the Continental United States NORAD Region. "Not since George Washington have we had a military commander in charge of U.S. forces in garrison at home to defend American citizens. It was a swift action by our government and president to guard our country from further terrorist attack."

McKinley, who assumed command from Maj. Gen. Larry K. Arnold in August 2002, says 1st Air Force and CONR are working closely with NORTHCOM to counter air threats as his Army and Navy counterparts protect land and sea.

Eberhart calls NORTHCOM a true joint venture. "Our command is built upon a Total Force and total national team concept that includes members from all five services; the National Guard; the Reserves; Department of Defense civilians; and numerous federal, state and local agencies," he says. "We believe we are redefining 'jointness' by forming new partnerships within the DOD and with numerous civilian agencies, as well as strengthening existing ones. Developing these strong relationships is key to our success." [7]

Eberhart says NORTHCOM is committed to improving "situational awareness by developing a common operating picture for the air, land and maritime domains." [8] McKinley and his team at 1st Air Force and CONR share that commitment and are working toward better command and control, a bigger radar picture and enhanced sensor capabilities to counter airborne threats. The 21st century is here and McKinley is leading the charge to catapult the air defense mission out of the Cold War into a new era, where the war seems to be everywhere.

Airman 1st Class Brian Isaacson, munitions maintenance specialist, 148th Fighter Wing, Minnesota Air National Guard, checks a gantry support leg on a munitions assembly conveyer on Jan. 23, 2002. Isaacson was one of hundreds of traditional Guardsmen activated to maintain the unit's increased operations tempo while supporting Operation Noble Eagle. The 148th is one of 10 Air National Guard fighter wings assigned to 1st Air Force and the Continental United States NORAD Region. Several other air wings are attached to the command for Operation Noble Eagle.

Air National Guard photo by Master Sgt. Daniel J. Schlies

Right: A New York National Guardsman patrols the devastation in New York City Sept. 14, 2001. Operation Noble Eagle has been characterized by a strong military presence in the United States since the earliest days of the Sept. 11 terrorist attacks.

Below: An F-15 pilot assigned to the Florida Air National Guard 125th Fighter Wing flies a Combat Air Patrol mission.

Photo by Tech. Sgt. Mark Olsen, New Jersey Department of Military and Veterans Affairs Public Affairs

Photo courtesy of 125th Fighter Wing, Florida Air National Guard

Charting the future

A few days before Sept. 11, 2001, the future of continental air sovereignty was in serious doubt. As late as Sept. 8, discussions at the Air Force's highest levels called for dismantling NORAD's seven alert sites and command and control structure — the heart of the air sovereignty mission. [9]

"Our leaders were seeking to optimize our force posture, and there was no perceived threat," McKinley says. "That rationale was changed dramatically by the events of Sept. 11, when the terrorists sent a message that we are no longer safe in our homes."

The air war over America has been fought ever since. [10] The old days of continental air sovereignty — protecting America's air borders with jets on alert at a few strategic locations — are a distant memory. Operation Noble Eagle requires scores of military fighters on alert at several bases around the country. Radar and command and control capabilities have had to keep up with looking both inside and outside the United States as fighter jets patrol America's cities, key infrastructure and special security events. The mission has changed, and it appears the changes will continue indefinitely.

"We will take 1st Air Force from a 20th century organization designed to defend against a Cold War construct, to a 21st century organization that protects Americans, Canadians and possibly anybody in the Western Hemisphere," McKinley says. "We are charting what this organization is going to look like in 2008 while we continue to fight the air war over America.

"This vision began in late 2002 ... over the next five years we plan to implement change, develop doctrine and concepts of operations and actually see those things come to fruition. We hope to put in place the means to fund the equipment and facilities that would enable us to carry out this strategy."

McKinley envisions an organization that blends seamlessly into the rest of the Air Force and falls strictly in line with Air Force doctrine, the book on how the "Air Force organizes and employs aerospace power throughout the spectrum of conflict at the operational level." [11] He sees the Northeast and Southeast air defense sectors consolidating into one. The Western Air Defense Sector at McChord Air Force Base, Wash., and new Eastern Air Defense Sector, probably in Rome, N.Y., would employ the latest technology to view airspace over the contiguous 48 states and territories like the U.S. Virgin Islands and Puerto Rico.

"Technology will allow us to radically transform the way we see the air traffic over North America," McKinley says. "After Sept. 11, we received a new system that enables us to do a far more efficient

Photo courtesy of 144th Fighter Wing, California Air National Guard

A fighter pilot from the California Air National Guard 144th Fighter Wing is caught on camera. Air defense leaders are working to gain more jobs in America's fighter wings for those fighting the war on terror.

High-Altitude Airships are the wave of the future. The lighter-than-air surveillance platforms are in production at Lockheed Martin.

Courtesy of Lockheed Martin

job controlling, monitoring and identifying traffic, not only outside our borders, but inside. Once that system is purchased en masse, we have the ability to reform, reengineer and reshape ourselves into a doctrinally correct numbered air force."

"Our goal is to mirror our air forces in Europe and the Pacific," McKinley says. "We will employ military members from the active duty Air Force, Air National Guard and Air Force Reserve, and will present our forces the way the Air Force presents its forces everywhere."

A crucial part of the strategy is a bigger and stronger Air Operations Center, McKinley says. The AOC is where war plans for Operation Noble Eagle are written. Planning for the war on terror would continue at this super AOC of the future slated for Tyndall Air Force Base, Fla., operated by the 601st Air Operations Group. In the world of warfighting, Air Force doctrine calls for one AOC per theater, and since the first moments of Operation Noble Eagle, the United States has become its own theater of

war, McKinley says.

"The war on terror is a long haul," he says. "It's nothing short term. We'll be facing this terrorist threat for our lives and the lives of our children. We'll have to remain vigilant around the clock for many years and never get complacent and never believe we aren't vulnerable.

"This reorganization allows us to be a numbered air force, air operations group and an Air Force forces staff," McKinley says. "It means we can take good care of our people and design strategy and concepts of operation so we can prevent acts of terrorism rather than just respond to them. This vision allows us to present our force structure to the commander of Northern Air Forces the way combatant commanders present their forces throughout the Air Force.

"This is a vectored evolution vision, it isn't total transformation. We haven't created anything new. It's a more modern and efficient way of presenting forces to best meet the needs of the new century."

> *"The war on terror is a long haul. It's nothing short term. We'll be facing this terrorist threat for our lives and the lives of our children. We'll have to remain vigilant around the clock for many years and never get complacent and never believe we aren't vulnerable."*
> — Maj. Gen. Craig R. McKinley, 1st Air Force commander

Retired Col. William A. Scott, 1st Air Force director of plans, programs and requirements, says the mission is simply evolving with the changing times. "Now that NORTHCOM has stood up, our mission has been enlarged to include possible offensive operations and civil support missions," Scott says. "The 1st Air Force and CONR transformation is a continued evolution from our doctrinally correct organization today to a doctrinally correct organization of the future."

McKinley, meanwhile, wears more hats than ever. He serves as the Commander of Air Force Forces for the continental United States; the Area Air Defense Commander; and Joint Air and Space Component Commander, a title that captures the Air Force position that air and space power together create effects that cannot be achieved through either power alone.

Technical edge

Building a modern, futuristic air defense mission means taking full advantage of the latest technology, from "High-Altitude Airships" to ground-based interceptors capable of destroying Intercontinental Ballistic Missiles mid-flight.

"Everything we see today is based on radars

From left, Tech. Sgts. Clayton Lemons and Leonard Mosley of the 147th Fighter Wing engine shop, Texas Air National Guard, make repairs while deployed to Egg Harbor Township, N.J., in support of Operation Noble Eagle.

U.S. Air Force photo by Master Sgt. Tom Louis

and those radars are mounted on the ground," says Col. Mike Corbett, 1st Air Force and CONR vice commander. "But we can only see line of sight. The curvature of the earth keeps controllers from seeing low altitudes. So low-altitude threats like cruise missiles are not well detected by ground-based radars."

The mission should someday employ High-Altitude Airships, solar-powered blimps cruising around the atmosphere and feeding air pictures back to earth. The airships, already being studied by the U.S. Army, are bigger than a football field and would stay airborne for up to a year at a time, Corbett says.

Eberhart spoke before the House Armed Services Committee about this exciting technology and what it means for homeland security.

"The Office of the Secretary of Defense, the Missile Defense Agency, the United States Army, and NORAD are spearheading the effort to demonstrate the technical feasibility of an unmanned, untethered, long-duration HAA (High-Altitude Airship)," the general said in March 2003.

"The prototype airship will stay airborne for one month and carry a 4,000-pound payload. We expect the objective HAA to have the capability to stay airborne for up to a year and carry a payload greater than 4,000 pounds. A robust HAA capability would give warfighters persistent wide-area surveillance of the battle space against a full spectrum of air, land and sea threats."

First Air Force and CONR hope to combine airship technology with enhanced command and control capabilities by 2004, Corbett says. That's the same year the United States Missile Defense Agency and its counterparts hope to have a ballistic missile defense in place. [12]

Ground-based interceptors; sea-based interceptors; airborne laser aircraft; and land, sea and space-based sensors; are just part of the technology that will protect against ballistic missiles of all ranges, according to the Department of Defense. [13]

Above: Master Sgt. Jim Rice, 147th Fighter Wing, Texas Air National Guard, signals that an AIM-120 missile is ready for the rack on Dec. 19, 2001. Rice and more than 60 other Texas Air Guard members were deployed to the 177th Fighter Wing, New Jersey Air National Guard, Egg Harbor Township, in the early days of Operation Noble Eagle.

Right: Tech. Sgt. Wendell Hunte, 177th Fighter Wing, New Jersey Air National Guard aircraft generation squadron, performs a function check after installing an AIM-9 adapter and rail on an F-16 on Oct. 9, 2001. The aircraft was de-armed for maintenance after many Operation Noble Eagle flying hours.

U.S. Air Force photos by Master Sgt. Tom Louis

People first

Modern equipment may be critical in the war on terror, but it's the people performing the air defense mission who are most invaluable.

"The dedication, skill and patriotism of our people and the fact we've done this without a single mishap to date, is a remarkable testament to the great skill and loyalty of everyone out there doing this job," McKinley said in February 2003. "Since Sept. 11, they have done a remarkable job of securing our airspace against further attack."

By April 2003, American and Canadian military forces had flown more than 29,000 Operation Noble Eagle sorties in defense of critical infrastructure and population centers throughout North America. [14]

Many Operation Noble Eagle veterans are Air National Guardsmen who were recalled to active duty. "Operation Noble Eagle missions and aerospace warning and control takes people," Corbett said in March 2003. "To date those people have been mobilized and can only be mobilized for a two-year period."

"When it comes to command and control functions, through modernization, we think we can do it with the resources we had prior to Sept. 11," Corbett says. "But for the fighter wings out there doing the alert mission, that isn't the case. There is a real need for a significant number of additional people."

The command is working closely with the Air Staff and National Guard Bureau to create 900 more jobs in America's alert fighter wings, Corbett says.

But it isn't just the military fighting the war, McKinley says. "How we prosecute tracks of interest with our interagency partners is forever changed," the commander says. "We have become America's NATO. We are the centerpiece of that partnership and are working with agencies like the FBI and U.S. Customs just as our partners in

Europe work with various countries to defend NATO."

"We can't rest on our laurels," he adds. "We'll continue to be challenged. We haven't suffered a reattack, but that doesn't mean people aren't out there planning, plotting and strategizing against us. We must stay vigilant and focused and support the president of the United States and secretary of defense in the war on terrorism."

"Air sovereignty has changed forever," McKinley concludes. "Not in my lifetime will we ever see an opportunity to turn the wick down a bit. This will be a very, very lengthy process."

1 Jim Garamone, "Northern Command to Debut in October," *American Forces Information Service,* 17 April 2002, n.p.

2 Ibid, n.p.

3 Ralph E. Eberhart, press conference at Tyndall Air Force Base, Fla., 1 August 2002.

4 Eberhart, speech before House Armed Services Committee, United States House of Representatives, 13 March 2003.

5 Garamone, "Northern Command to Debut in October," n.p.

6 Ibid., n.p.

7 Eberhart, before Housed Armed Services Committee, 13 March 2003.

8 Ibid.

9 Dan Navin and William A. Scott, conversation with author, 16 April 2002.

10 As of press time in late-2003.

11 United States Air Force, *Organization and Employment of Aerospace Power* (Headquarters Air Force Doctrine Center, Maxwell Air Force Base, Ala., 2000), foreword.

12 Missile Defense Operations Announcement, *DOD News*, 17 December 2002, n.p.

13 Ibid., n.p.

14 NORAD statistics.

The "Tribute of Light" represents the fallen twin towers of the World Trade Center. The photograph was taken from Liberty State Park, N.J., March 14, 2002.

154

U.S. Air Force photo by Gary Ell